Just Because Life

Alicia Genna

iUniverse, Inc.
New York   Bloomington

iUniverse books may be ordered through booksellers or by contacting:

iUniverse
1663 Liberty Drive
Bloomington, IN 47403
www.iuniverse.com
1-800-Authors (1-800-288-4677)

ISBN: 978-1-4502-2864-0 (sc)
ISBN: 978-1-4502-2865-7 (ebook

Printed in the United States of America

iUniverse rev. date: 05/27/2010

Prologue

I would like to take you through my childhood. It's the most important part of our development but also what we carry around with us for the rest of our lives. It's the time we reflect upon when situations come up or memories prevail. But not everyone has the same, or we would be clones, which makes everyone unique in their own way. I wish I could start at an early age, such as 4 or 5 but my memory only takes me to 6 or 7 and even that is shaded pretty dark. Later on you will realize why and understand how powerful the human mind can be, especially in the sense of survival.

Going back to early childhood

I remember nothing about elementary school, and I sorely wish I did, for I have heard others speak of their memories and I have nothing to give back. But at the same time I realize that it wasn't that important for me because it was a very fragile time.

I lived with my mother and father in a two story home. They were called attached houses which I always thought was ridiculous but some builder thought otherwise. The odds of my mother being around were very slim in which I say I grew up mostly with my father . Most of my lessons and trials learned, came from him. He started me at a young age, although I don't remember with clarity, I can say by six I could change the oil on a car. I could help build a tire swing, help with the house, work with wood and nails, swing a hammer without missing the mark, and handle the steering wheel of a car while I sat on my Dad's lap. At six years old I would say that's quite a lot of accomplishments, but I don't remember being happy about any of them.

I was a girl so I should have been girly right? I've always wondered if things would have been different in the aspect of my father not being ill as I was told, if I would have turned out different or the same. I'll let you decide on the way.

I remember at seven I was next door at my friends house. They didn't live there very long, but the girl was about my age so we became friends fast. Unfortunately the only thing I remember about her was her Cat and how badly I wanted one. A few weeks down the line her cat had a litter and I was so excited because I was going to bring one home. So when they were ready to be weaned from the mother I stole one while no one was looking, snuck it under my shirt and walked casually home. Its so funny to look back and remember it, like a scene from a movie as it rolls through my mind.

As I was walking home I saw my dad outside and thought uh-oh! There was no way to by-pass him to get into the house . He was working on his car and seemed pretty intense so I kept on walking. Than I heard "Alicia" in a normal tone and walked back panicking. He acted so normal I thought I was okay, but the cat under my shirt got onto my back somehow and was clawing at me. I kept wondering if he could see it. We had a normal conversation, him asking how hanging with my friend was and other just random questions. I realize now what I didn't than, how he was biding his time to let me say something about the cat instead of him calling me out on it. So finally I blurted out "I stole the cat from next door and it's a kitten and she was so cute and I have to have her Daddy! Please don't make me go back!" he started laughing. And this is when I got my lesson on stealing.

He explained to me how the neighbors must feel searching for the poor kitten thinking it got lost. How panicked and scared they were and all the while the kitten was safe, they had no idea of knowing that. He told me the adult thing to do was face the fear of embarrassment and explain why I did what I did. I didn't get the embarrassment until he walked me over and I had to face the parents and do the explaining. I was horrified! Needless to say they told my father that if I really wanted the kitten and if it was okay with him, that I could take her home. I must've jumped 10 feet high I was so happy. I looked up at him and when he saw my face I guess it was all the persuasion that I needed. I got my kitten and named her Fluffy.

It was times like those I love to roll the images in my mind. Not only are they refreshing, but they make you realize why parents do the things they do as well as how much love a person can have for you. I think we take that for granted way to often and should recognize it more.

The great thing about getting that kitten was she had a twin. I don't know for sure if that is possible with animals, but my best friend Shay Brickel at that time had gotten the brother of the cat and they looked exactly alike. His mother Laurie told me they were twins of the litter and Shay and I were in awe. We were really excited about that. His mom had so many cats when I was young. I thought it was so cool except every time we would hang out at his house I would have an allergy attack. But I never stopped going over there.

Me and Shay grew up together. It was said we were born in the same hospital and our parents knew each other since our births. Ever since we could talk we never were apart unless we had to be. My father loved Shay like a son. He was fond of his family and always had surprises for us. He would take us on sleigh rides at the park when the snow was there. It was always a great time. I remember a time where Shay and I rode the sleigh down that mountain and hit a huge mound, flew over and went right into a tree. Was hilarious than and now! My father came running down worried, than realized we were okay. we couldn't stop laughing for hours, it was great. He also had built us a little tree house in the back to let our imaginations be wild. We used to pretend to be business people which was ironic, since I think it was meant to be child wild. Space ships, or maybe a pirate ship, but we always had more adult ideas. We were too smart for our own good.

A couple years later I believe I was nine or ten I became a woman. Now like I said my mother really wasn't in the picture so when mother nature hit, I had to call my dad over and it was weird. I was scared though from the blood so I didn't care, I thought I was dying. He told me what had happened and explained the way a women's system is. The whole time the only thing I could think was Not Fair! So I told him "what! I want to be a boy than. This is not good I don't want it." I always made him laugh as he often made me laugh, but I never saw the humor than. When they say "time heals all things and unveils all motives" I know the true meaning of it and appreciate the saying.

After all that mess with becoming a woman I still was the same tom boy I wanted to be. My fathers best friend, Bob Seaman, had a son, Jason. We were supposed to be friends. Well I didn't like Jason. He was to passive I think at that time. I was all rough and tough so I gave him a hard time every time he came over. If there is one thing I can say I remember is hating Barbie's or dolls altogether! For Christmas one year he gave me a mermaid Barbie and I was so mad. I hated it and I ripped it's head off. Its what I did to all the Barbie's that I was given. I guess it was a statement that didn't get across to well because I still got Barbie's.

Poor guy, I'm sure I did worst to him but unfortunately I cannot remember.

Just a girl

All my friends were boys. We all lived in the neighborhood and grew up together. I was the only girl so I was just considered one of them. It was fun growing up that way because we would play basketball with the hoop my dad had built, or baseball in the street. We played every sport really and hiked adventures in the woods past our back yards. We just about pissed off every adult in that neighborhood and loved every minute of it.

On the weekends my dad and I would go to Hi-Tor shelter and do some volunteer work. I used to be in love with the manager there because he was so nice to me and never looked at me like a kid, but like a young adult and I felt proud. One weekend, while walking past the kennels, I looked over and spotted a beautiful dog with enough sadness in her eyes to make your heart hurt. I immediately knew that I had to have this dog. It felt like life or death. I never understood it than or maybe I did and I didn't want to but it will come to light later on.

I went and got my father and brought him to her kennel and said "Dad, I Have to have her. it's a matter of life and death and I will die if I don't bring her home." than did the begging that a kid does when they want something. I fought tooth and nail that day to win her but he wouldn't budge. Even said my mom wouldn't have it. I thought to myself who cares! Which sounds horrible, but I didn't care. She was never there anyway. As we were leaving I was still begging and crying. We got in the car and I just went mute. My heart hurt for that dog. I knew we needed each other and there was nothing I could do.

The next day I got home from school, I got off the bus and ran home. When I got to the door and opened it I heard barking. I looked at the top of the stairs and there she was. The dog I needed and who needed me was sitting there waiting for me with her tongue hanging out. She was beautiful. They say she was a golden retriever, collier mix, but to me she was a princess and so sprang her name. I called for my dad and he came from the kitchen with a huge smile on his face. All I could do was smile back. I was bursting with happiness and pride that my father got me the dog I so desperately wanted. Now the funniest part was when my mom came in from work later that night. It was late, and I was in bed. I heard growling and mad barking. I was scared at first than realized Princess didn't know my mom and she wasn't letting her in the house!

I was giggling like crazy and I heard my father laugh before he went to get her. Than I listened to the conversation between them. My mother yelling "what the hell is that and what is it doing here" and my father telling her the story. It was mostly my mother screaming at my dad, not an unusual thing, but I got mad because he didn't tell her what he did for me just that he got the dog at the shelter. That was it. I didn't know why, but I hated my mother for being so mean to him especially at times like that when he would do something for me. She got over it, she had to and ended up in love with the dog herself. But not as much as Princess and my dad loved each other. He would sit in his chair in front of the Television and eat peanuts with her. One for me one for you type thing and I thought it was funny. They had such a close bond. We did too, but her and my dad, it was unexplainable, but I think because my father brought her home and out of the kennel, she felt he was her savior. I also feel because of the trauma she had gone through before she landed in that shelter she was healing and my Dad helped her do that. He trained her with respect and loyalty. I loved her just as much but we had a friendship bond as "lets go play."

I learned that the relationships formed, no matter with who or what, always deserve respect and loyalty. Without it you have no foundation to build on.

Your probably wondering at this point where all the grief had taken place with all the good memories I've given you. Well with good there always come bad and that's how it was for me. I just hold the good memories close to my heart and let the bad ones go, but I will give you an idea of what the other side was like.

Diagnosis

They say my father was Bipolar. Nobody ever told me that until I was older ,so you can imagine how I felt. I grew up not knowing why my father was wonderful one day and terrifying the next. No one had the nerve or the gall to sit me down and explain it, they let me just endure it and I will always remember that till the day I lay at eternal rest. It's not something you take lightly.

I had three brothers. Brian being the oldest, David being second oldest and Cary being older than me but the youngest. Brian was off to college when I was growing up, and I never knew where David was. I think he too was in college or living somewhere else but they both feared my father, I know that. And some how that gives me enough satisfaction to let the past of them go. Cary was a whole other story. He was always getting in trouble and hanging with the wrong people. Funny he was the smartest, best looking and most fun, yet I didn't get to know him that well. He was in and out of jail, but we will get back to him later. The reason I bring my brothers into this is because as I have explained to them, at some point of their life during all this, they could have stepped out of their box and helped. Not only do I believe that but I know how true it is and how selfish and demanding they are. If it's not to benefit them they didn't get involved. And with that I went through days where I prayed I would die.

Most days I didn't want to go home because I didn't know what I was going to face. Would he be mad? Would he be in a trance? Pacing, happy, sad? It was a lotto every time I got off the bus.

There were times where we would do my homework and I would get whipped when I got something wrong or didn't understand. And that happened a lot. I wasn't a fast learner but under that pressure it made it really hard to concentrate, let alone learn. Than there were times he wouldn't answer at all to my calls. He would mow the lawn ten times like he kept forgetting he did it or he would fly into a rage and whip me to the point of scars. But all those different emotions he experienced was not him. That wasn't my father and as I know that now from so much studying and schooling, back than I was turning to hate him

I would beg my mother to do something, anything to make it stop, but she had no answers. She would coddle me some nights read me a book or two but that was it. It wasn't enough. Or she would fly in to a rage with my dad in an argument and grab me to leave. We would walk and walk with no destination. Than there were times I saw her violent side come out. She would shove him down the stairs, or start hitting him, just outrageous things a kid should not see. My father was not a small man. He was over 6'2' and my mother is 5'0' so you can imagine the fear that would crawl in me when she would fight like that. But not once did my father ever lift a hand to her. There lesson there for me; a real man never hit's a woman and a real woman never hit's a man.

What baffles me is no one will speak of my fathers past. When he was young. What he was like, what he did for fun. I have always wondered, who was my father besides the man I knew. My brothers won't tell me the relationship they had with him and at that time he was not sick. I envy them for that but I also feel bad for them because to me they are wimps when it comes to dealing with things. They can't handle it but to cut off people from their lives. Cary was a different story, but I don't know the background on that either as no one will speak of it. I have only what I remember and the stories I have learned over the years.

The Tragedy

My mother and I had gone to see my brother Cary in Syracuse a few weeks before. I was too young to wonder why they talked through plastic on a phone, it was stupid I thought. But I remember hearing divorce from his mouth. The only thing I remember from that trip and never thought about it than. Didn't even know really what I meant. But I was soon to find out.

My father committed suicide on August 11, 1995. I was a witness to the act, but I was "supposed" to be prepared for it. I just didn't understand than. I was too young to so I don't blame myself, but now it settles my mind. And I will describe the events of that day that led up to that last minute.

That day, on August 11, 1995, I woke up feeling strange. I remember because I thought I was sick, but knew I wasn't. During that day it seemed as though my dad was on a mission. He was all over the place, upstairs, downstairs, garage, sheds, just going around like a whirlwind making my head spin. Finally he gathered me into the car, said we were going to my Grandma's house. During that time it was normal because we were always going to some family members house so I thought nothing of it.

We got there and my dad rushed my grandma into getting ready to go and packed. He told her he was taking her back to our house and than we were going to Massachusetts to see my brother for the weekend. She put up a bit of a fight but my dad won most arguments with anyone so it didn't last and we were on our way back home.

When we got home he was back to doing the strange running around the house and I was waiting for my mother to get home. I believe he called her but I don't remember the conversation they had. Next thing I knew my mom was there and so were the cops . I never like the cops because growing up I feel as though they were there more often or not, trying to get my dad out. What I didn't know was that my mom called them a lot to get him into a psychiatric center. To me, this all felt wrong.

They were making my dad leave and my mom was enforcing it. She said she got an order of protection and he was not to be at the house or anywhere around it. She proceeded to say she was filing for a divorce. I watched my father's face, and realized he knew, but I still saw how he broke inside. His eyes, my eyes were expressive enough to know without words. And I knew than that's when a piece of both my father and I died.

All I wanted was for all of what the family was going through to end. And I felt then and there that I got my prayer, or wish and I couldn't do anything other than cry. Its not what I really wanted, I was just scared and didn't know what else to ask for. The police tried to grab me to calm me down because I would start yelling at them but I never let them catch me. It was the Haverstraw Police department in Pomona New York and to this day I still have problems with them. They never gave my family a break.

My father didn't put up a fight like he always did. It seemed like he just gave up. The look on his face is the look that still haunts me now and again, one of complete failure and sadness as he walked away from me. He didn't take his car though, he took my mothers. I didn't see a big deal, but apparently it was to her.

I remember that too because of the snit she put up about it. My grandmother was a mess and fighting with my mother and I sat by the window waiting. I felt numb and don't know why but I knew he would come back. He was my daddy and I was his princess. He wouldn't have left me, he always told me he would never leave me.

After things died down a little I saw him pull up at the curb. I ran out to him. I was so happy he came home and kept asking him what was happening. He told me to go and tell my mom that we would make this last trip to Massachusetts to see my brother, than he would do what she wanted him to do.

So me; I just cared about him being there and getting the family together, I ran in and told her. She kept saying no, so I kept begging and begging. Finally she gave in, and I ran out to tell him.

He packed up the car. It was weird how he did it though. Behind his seat was everybody's bags and so on. We had a white Ford Taurus wagon. He put princess in the back, she went everywhere we did, than made my mom sit in the middle, and me behind my grandmother, who sat in the passenger seat up front. We were about to leave when he said he needed coffee. My mom said she would get it, him not being allowed in, but he got out and went in anyway. Something I hold against my mom to this day as well is she knew. That whole time she knew why he went inside. While I knew sub-consciously I was still to young to really understand. It was sometime before he got back, but we were on our way.

About two hours or so into the drive he said he was tired and we had to turn around and go home. My mother freaked and told him she would drive the rest of the way. He fought her about it and finally she gave up. I was clinging to her at this point because I felt scared. Actually I was terrified. Everything was so wrong and becoming worse by the second I couldn't breathe right and I felt as though the world was ending. Little did I know, a part of it was about to.

We pulled into my neighborhood, but instead of parking in the driveway, he pulled to the curb around the bend of the court we lived in. He looked in the rearview mirror with a look of defeat and submission and said it was time for him to go. The next thing I knew I heard ringing in my ears and nothing else. It was like going deaf. After a few seconds I heard my grandmother screaming as though she got hurt and my mother yelling to go in and call for help. Nobody moved but than I looked over at my dad one more time and something in me panicked, so I bolted out of the car and ran. Just ran and ran.

I saw the paramedics, cops, and my mother with my dog crying at the curb. I couldn't go near them though.

That was the night I had seen too much for a child , and grew up too fast with too much wisdom on my shoulders.

Still Going

I never really got over the ordeal with my dad. I made myself let it go but it built in me through the years affecting me in little ways I didn't care to notice. I held on to memories and never forgave myself for not being able to do anything. I hated my mother for making all that happen and my brothers began to become enemies.

I went though the years in a trance. In school I was tortured with words because everyone knew what had happened. It was all over the papers and the parents had told their kids I was crazy, to stay away from me because of it. So I had no one. No friends, except the ones I already had, but even they weren't themselves around me. But I got through and didn't really care about anything. I began smoking cigarettes, playing with drugs, and constantly getting in trouble. I talked back and I acted out often. I would say I wanted attention but everyone was so blind to it, they didn't see anything but a trouble maker.

A turn of time

I was 13 when I went to California. I loved it. The weather, the people I met, everything about it because it wasn't Rockland. Nobody knew me, my dad, what happened, nothing. No judgment, just freedom. I made good friends there, my best friend being Laura and second being Annaliese. I miss them both dearly today in fact. They were my two first Real girl friends. We did so much and had great times.

My Uncle Vito, I believe, held a grudge towards my mother. He always had something negative to say about her and he looked at me always as if I was a liar and scum. I hated it but he was worth nothing to me. My Aunt Adrianna was another one that meant nothing. She was a lying hypocrite. But still their staring and judgment on me and my mom started catching up.

I became a cutter. I never thought to hide it though for some reason. Maybe I wanted help, or maybe I just didn't care, but I used any razor I could find and I used it on my arms. Smart enough never to do it on a vein or on my wrists. It was the pain I wanted, not and ending.

To explain it, when you cause pain or are in pain, your body starts producing adrenaline and endorphins to help numb it as a natural defense. And when you extend that pain the more is produced. It was like a high. I also like to see the blood because as emotionless as I felt, the blood reminded me that I was indeed alive, and that I was only human.

After a while my uncle realized what I was doing and swore I was trying to commit suicide. He never was that bright to my thinking and he was heartless as well. He sent me to a therapist threatening me to put me in an institution if I ever did it again. It scared me a little but I grew so much hate for him I didn't care all that much.

So here came the therapist. If you haven't seen the movie "Good Will Hunting" I recommend it. I wasn't to far off from the description in that movie and I made every therapist I went to hate me. They tried putting me on pills all the time and it was annoying. I always outwitted them and when I had them thinking they were about to get somewhere with me, I would let them know they failed. The whole thing was a waste of time and very annoying.

Than my Uncle harassed me about having an eating disorder. It was hilarious because I ate more than them and my cousins all together, but they swore I ate nothing ever. It was pathetic and still is to this day how they tried to label me with something, anything. The reason, so they didn't look so bad themselves. My aunt was a drunk who snuck cigarettes, my uncle swore to the church but was anything but a saint. My cousin Amanda was young and naive, my cousin Vincent was at the "transition" stage of boy becoming man and used me sometimes. What did he do to me? I'll never say, but when my aunt finally had an idea that something was going on, she blamed me. She said I had a crush on him and wouldn't budge from her thinking. It was a joke to me and I didn't fight it because she too was a joke. I look at her today and I pity the whole family. Amanda made it out okay. But the fact that she didn't stay in touch hurt. I covered for her. Vincent used her as well once in a horrible way that she didn't tell me about until the drama my Aunt created was out. I wanted to fight for her and she begged me not to tell. Well cheers Amanda and here's to silence.

It was definitely an interesting year and a half. I missed my friends, still do, but it wasn't worth the aches and pains that part of the family caused. I should have known it being my dad's brother, that things wouldn't have worked out.

Sentiment

What I don't want to do is make this a step by step about me. There are a great many things I will leave out and many I will put in. but none of it will be sequenced. I want it as I lived it, with nothing in sequence, but always out of whack.

Its enough to give you a sense that no matter what, we still have the opportunity to make what we want to be our future ours. You just have to be willing to fight for it.

The beginning of love, laughter and grief

After a trip to Italy with the whole immediate family, I came back refreshed and ready to start over. It was 1998 and I was 15. And the most memorable part of my life happened that year. I met my first love. Brian Patrick Hansen. He was 18 and had redneck all over him, but we loved each other with ever thing we had. He was my first and I his. We experienced so much together and he always had a shoulder for me. We never had to be fake and we fought like couples did, but nonetheless, nothing could ever come between us. Or so I thought.

In 1999 some things were starting to happen to me that I couldn't understand. There would be times I couldn't breathe and would black out. Than times were I thought my heart was going to pound out of my chest and breathing was terrifying. All the while I started to withdrawal from everything and everyone because I started becoming scared of leaving the house. During the time I couldn't tell Brian. I was ashamed, embarrassed and I didn't know what was happening to me. So he told me he couldn't see me any more. I believe that's what brought me over the edge.

Everything was getting worse. I didn't leave the house or I cried all the time. Thinking it was depression from him not being with me anymore, I didn't tell anyone. But than one night it became the night of my worst fears.

I slept on the couch, always did, not sure why, but it was my spot. I was lying down getting ready to sleep when my heart started pounding horribly. Stronger than I ever felt it. It was like it was everywhere at once. Than my vision started blurring and my breathing shortened. I called for my mother. I couldn't make much sound but I kept calling. She finally heard me and ran over to me. She realized I couldn't breath or talk so she called 911 panicking. I thought, swore, I was dying. It was starting to get black when the phone rang and I heard Brian's voice on the other end with my mom. He heard it on his scanner, the 911 call, and was worried. Hearing his voice calmed it all a little but I still couldn't catch a breath for the life of me. Long story short, after being in the hospital and all tests saying I was okay I knew that in my world, it wasn't going to be okay.

I met the psychiatrist assigned to the hospital and that was when therapy and drugs were going to be a permanent part of my life. The list of disorders was insane and all because of one event that I chose to ignore. One event, and the years I was carrying it around finally snapped my brain into attention. It was saying it needed rest and relief.

I remembered all that time in California with all the therapists, and none of them even coming close to what I was learning I had. I came to the realization that I was protecting myself without even knowing it and if I would have believed them I would have been in big trouble. All they knew was the story my Uncle or Aunt told them because I never would say anything but mind screw them, and with that they thought I was far worse than what it was.

I had Depression, PTSD (post traumatic stress disorder) and an anxiety disorder than ranged from general to social, depending on what situation I was in. I realized they all melted into one, and all from watching my father die. I know why I didn't face it, and I still didn't, but I couldn't live the way I was going so I sought the help I needed.

I met a lady who changed my life. She was the first person who I didn't want to lie to, or pretend . She was homely and comforting and didn't force. She just sat there and when I didn't want to talk, she didn't make me, which eventually led me to talking. Dr. Beverly Lipson was amazing and was more friend than psychologist. She gave me hope and a new outlook. My psychiatrist, world known, author and extraordinaire, Dr. Peter Birkett, was the man who believed me and believed in me, which gave me hope as well. I feared and sometimes still do that I would get what my father had. But he always gave me reassurance and made me realize I'm just me, and I'm ok. I suffered a traumatic event. I was being normal, but my mind and body needed to hash it out. Keeping to myself was destroying me, hence the panic attacks.

So I learned than that no matter what, you can keep so much to yourself, but we do explode eventually and never in the same way. My way was through reliving the event and panicking at seeing or hearing certain things that had relation to it or my father. I got through the PTSD and Depression because I realized that you can't fight it. It fights back harder and wins every time. So I let go and released everything, all the pain I built and all the years of hiding it. It was a relief, on mind and body. I would wish no one to go through what I did.

Years being thrown away

So from there on out, I still lived the same way. I just did what I had to do, with the visits and pills if I started to feel the panic. I felt better and was getting stronger every day. It wasn't easy or comfortable, but I still used drugs here and there, smoked too many cigarettes or drank too much. So nothing at that point was good for me.

Than I really turned my life upside down for the worst. Albert Jason Hickey. AJ was the most sought after guy in school and all through high school and had more girls than the normal good looking guy. But he wanted me and I felt, well excited. This guy, the "bad boy" wanted me. So I dated him. I'll never forget the phone call that ruined us both.

He called me one night and was very panicky. Eventually he told me he was in love with me. And than I lied. I told him I loved him too. Seemed like it was only right. I was his first love and he's been with almost every girl in the Rockland area, so what else was I supposed to say.

But ever since that call we drifted and became more enemies than anything else. I couldn't even look at him. Sex was not in the equation. Every time we tried I wanted to die because of the guilt I felt. And all the while when we officially broke everything off, I realized I hated him. I had more disgust than desire because I saw what and who he really was. This one guy, who was a user to women, who was also a drug addict and cheater made me feel as though I was nothing more than "that other girl." And even when I was with him I felt cheap. He was the guy everyone wanted but the man I despised.

I could only imagine his reaction when he finally learns the truth. All these years later I'm able to say things and put them into the perspective they need to be put in. He's happy now with his wife, a girl who always hated me, Michelle, and I believe he has a son. I'm happy he finally made a life for himself. I even tried to call once and tell him that to lose some of that disgust I still felt, but because his wife hated me I couldn't get to him. So I pretended to be someone else. Than he was rude to me on the phone making it sound as if he were to good to talk to me. The laugh I had over that with my friends was relieving, and I realized than, people never change. We are who we are and always will be. You can't change someone and they can't change you. So the disgust was gone and he no longer had a place. I got what I needed but I did feel bad. I tried becoming a friend but he rejected this, which I know was more his wife than anything. And that was that. I said Good bye to a memory I wished never existed.

People ask others all the time, "do you have regrets?" I hear most of them say no. This is observation. I've myself been asked and lied saying no myself. But I figured out why. I regret so much of my past because I didn't have the knowledge than I do now, which isn't fair to use, but I do. I wish a lot of the things I did could be rectified, corrected, changed. I hated who I was, how I was, what I became. But I never really had a place because I couldn't figure out for certain who I wanted to be. I couldn't find me with so much being stirred around me. So do I have regrets? Yes, so many I could make a book of that itself. in the end I come to my solution, if I change one piece, just one, of any part of my life and I wouldn't be sitting here writing this, helping others with the knowledge and power I have to help them, and I would not have my son. So therefore "everything happens for a reason" is a blessed quote to me.

My Blood, turned into water

I just turned 16 when I lost my brother Cary. He was well known in Rockland, for being in the wrong places at the wrong times. His rap sheet could have sheltered many and his life was always being shattered by the wrong people.

My brother was the smartest out of the family besides my father. His IQ was astounding and he always was the A student (when he attended.) I remember him getting on the Deans list one year as well. But he never had a straight path or enough time to make one. I won't say he never tried, he did. But "losers" always found him to join their path.

I remember a story my mother once told me. She was waiting for him to come home one night and he was thrown on our lawn. When she went out to him he was bleeding from every pore of his body. He over dosed and she believes he had a seizure as well. My mother fought hard for my brother. Whatever he needed she gave. Whenever he needed she was there. And wherever he was she went. He and I were the only ones as I explained who lived with my father when he got ill. He escaped though and just ran. He couldn't handle it. My brother loved my father dearly. He used to tell me our father was like a scientist with his knowledge but a firecracker with his emotions. I used to laugh at that. The whole time my brother drank and did drugs to make sure he knew and felt nothing. And all the while my brothers stood by knowing this, did nothing. I could only imagine the sweat and blood my mother dripped fighting to save him. Having my own child has made that clearer for me, but even than I watched her. And my brothers never helped her once. It was disgusting to me, so I tried in any way I could and crossed off my brothers as blood and made them water.

The times he was home, though very seldom, were so much fun. He taught me to break dance, fight and use self-defense, and taught my friends and I to blow hearts with our cigarettes. He was huge on music. He knew every Michael Jackson move, lyrics to so many songs and wrote his own a lot. He shared some with me and I have to say he did have talent. He spoke from the heart and he was a lot like Motley Crew. Being it was his favorite band, I think they inspired him. I still listen to their music but my favorite songs are when he turned into Sixx A.M. Nikki Sixx left an impression with my brother, and his song "Life is Beautiful," has left and impression on me. I hear it at least once a day and I know, it will be okay. I believe it's fair to say that we relate our lives to songs, music and words. If not our own than someone else's. To find relation is like finding peace and consolation.

There wasn't anyone who disliked my brother. Those either loved him or feared him as he was a big guy, skinny yes, but his height scared very many. And when he fought he made sure he fought well and so that the other never got back up. He made me proud in many ways. When I needed someone he would come. There were nights he slept on our roof and I would sneak him pillows and blankets. Or times he would just appear like smoke to just talk to me. About everything and nothing, we made it though, in our own way and got to know each other our own way. He always told me I was his best girl and I always loved him.

On august 26, 2000 my brother died. The whole thing was horrid. Nobody knew what really happened until I went back later to find out, but the call came in as he committed suicide in his cell. The truth being he was killed by his guards, witnessed by a man in the cell next to his own. He had witnessed the whole thing and how it was covered up. He wrote me and we kept going back and forth until I made sense of it.

If there was one thing, one person I knew in this life, it was my brother. He would talk but he never would go through with it. Never. And through tooth and nail and hunting down old friends and talking to the mates in cells around him I got the truth I already knew, but had to leave it as is for many reasons. One was to keep my mother breathing. The other was because knowing was enough for me and I believe it was enough justice for him to know I uncovered it. So in the papers again, Cary Genna committed suicide following his fathers footsteps.

Somewhere out there is his daughter. I don't know who she is, how old or where, but he bore a baby girl. He was proud of that and tattooed her name on his arm. I have tried very hard to find her, but my leads didn't get me very far. I believe that if, by chance she picks this up, she might know now that there is one more person in this life that loves her. She is my niece and nothing changes that. Blood is blood. Unless it runs like water.

Losing my brother was by far the hardest thing I have felt in my life. It was as if everything in me was ripped out. I suffered for my dad, but was too young to truly know or understand. But for my brother I knew too much and suffered very badly. I still to this day have very thin nerves when his name is mentioned. He was a big and small part of my life. As he wasn't always there, when he was he made an impact. He was my rock and now my rock was six feet under.

It took a long time for me to come to terms with that. He being buried with my father was the best thing though. They needed each other and now, they rest together. And they both live in my heart and help me through this life. I am very lucky in a cruel world, where most would see me as misfortunate. But I had what I needed. I felt the love some never experience and know the two best men of my life are with me everyday. There's no greater gift.

Gray Areas

There is so much in between the lines, but that's my "gray" area. I'm giving you the black and white so you understand that no matter what, there is a gray area where you make your own. That you make your path, choose your choices and live how you wish to live. There have been so many complications in mine, but all in all its still mine to live and build. And that "gray" area I will keep for me. Some of my struggles, and fights. Its what made me who I am.

As I mentioned earlier I will not make this a step by step of me. I'm giving you the will and the knowledge to realize that no matter what, there is no such thing as "it is what it is." it is a simple saying that could mean basically anything. It IS what you make it, and it will be what you want it to be if you fight hard enough for it. I've fought some battles I was told by professional doctors I would lose and yet maybe I am a medical miracle, but I believe that I gave it all I had and I came through with determination. And that's what life is. The need to understand the balance, the Ying and Yang, the good from evil, and gain the strength from all your journeys.

"GOD never said it would be easy. HE said it would be worth it."

The Move

In 2002 I moved to Las Vegas, Nevada and turned a new leaf, made a new path. I did what I wanted to do, had to do, and accomplished a lot doing so. I had no drama to deal with and met good people on the way. When you leave where your from and known, and go somewhere your never heard of, you get that chance to be who you are and not have a worry in the world. And that's what I did. I was able to be me. To live happy and accomplish things I never would have here. Nothing was perfect, but I made the right choice in moving and did the best I could on my path.

For my circumstances I can say I came out a winner with far more respect for myself in which I finally recognized and deserve. I had a great friend the entire time and occasional good friends here and there. It was hard with my husband at the time to keep friends, or even being allowed to have them.

The Husband

I had just turned 19 when I met Richard Joseph Works, and he was 21. We met at DMV on Friday, September 13, 2002

When I first met Rich, I fell in love. I never believed in the whole "love at first sight," but with him that's basically how it happened. Later that night, we decided to go out. I was very nervous, I just met this random guy, at the DMV no less, but at the same time I had this feeling with him that I trusted so I went with it. Needless to say I met his younger brother and Aunt as well before we went out.

We walked the strip, which was a good few miles, but it didn't feel like we walked at all. More like floating. We talked about everything. He told me about him, his past and I told him about me and mine. It was so nice to have someone to talk to. We ended up staying together until the early morning, and all we did was talk. I knew I was in love and it felt really good.

I think at the time, because of his history he was just getting back on his feet and things with us had moved way to quickly. I ended up living with him at his Aunt's house which felt natural. I helped take care of his brother and I tutored him with his studies. At the same time I was going to college myself. We were doing really well.

During all this time I like to think, or hope maybe, that he wasn't on drugs and that he was okay. He didn't show any abusive patterns and we fought, but like couples do. But we loved each other enough to get through everything.

I'm not sure what happened or when it happened, but our relationship started falling apart. He had left me once during it to be back with his ex- wife. That broke my heart and was hard to deal with, but in the end I won him back. But after that we were never the same. I was never comfortable anymore and the trust was pretty much gone on my end. But I went on, I didn't know any better, all I knew was that I loved him and that was all that mattered.

We got married on May 7, 2004 and it was beautiful. Before we got married we had a lot of problems that we never worked through and I believe it was another add on to the stress of us. Our honeymoon was a disaster and I paid for everything down to the rings. We ended up living together in our own house and things started to get worse.

A few months after we married I was pregnant. I was so excited and thought maybe this is our chance. Unfortunately it didn't work like that. He was not happy about it and wanted me to abort it. I tried talking to my mom about it but even she said to abort it. My own mother! She proceeded to tell me she had wanted to abort me and if not for my father she would have. My feelings for her were gone, whatever was left at least. I always knew I wasn't wanted by her, but to hear her say it straight out the way she did was like experiencing another death in my heart. When it came down to it, Rich left me no choice. He dropped me off at the clinic and made me abort the child. I begged them not to and told them I didn't want to do it but they went ahead because they got their money. I was never the same after that, Rich knew that too. Another piece of me died that day, literally though and I never will forgive myself for that. I even knew it was a boy. I pray and light candles, but how do you penance a death you let happen? Its something I will live with until I pass on. I always like to think that Nathan might have been that little boy, and God gave me the chance once more to have him. It's a far stretched hope, but its still hope.

Out of our relationship the friends I made would come and go, none wanting to be around him or would give me the ultimatum of him or them. And It made sense. I wasn't really allowed to have friends. He hated when I was with others and raged about that too. I wish I could say he wasn't abusive, but he was. More verbally than physically. But both are wrong and I should have left him but I couldn't.

I feel like I should have known better but how was I supposed to. My family hated him, but hell, they hated me so what was the difference! We made do for a while, but he would up and leave and be gone for more time they he would be around. I think that was the point when he started doing drugs again. Another thing I should have known, and a small part of me did, but when I approached the matter he would go into a rage. Same with cheating. which I knew he was doing as well.

I met two wonderful people out of it, his close friend Paul, and Paul's girlfriend Lindsay. Paul was a sweetheart in every way and Lindsay became a best friend. I loved them both and we would have great times together. But other than that I was dealing with his anger, spitting rage in my face and the times I defended myself, I went to jail for it. Twice he put me in jail even though every time I made him look like a gentleman and we just had an argument like couples do.

I divorced him in 2005 but we still stayed together up until my son was born. That was it for me. I knew for sure than he was cheating, doing drugs and only God knows what else and I walked away free and clear. My son and I were free and that's all that mattered.

I won't lie and say I don't still love him. I would go to safe houses and do testimonials about what I went through and how I got to the point that I could walk away. I had vows with him, and whether it meant something to him or not, it meant something to me. That's why I kept trying and did all I could do. And that is why when I walked away the final time it was like a heavy weight was lifted off my chest and heart. I was okay and I knew that. That in no way was I to blame for anything, and in the end I did everything I could. He chose his path and I chose mine. It's better this way because I feel Nathan needs all of me and I have what it takes to raise him the way he needs to be raised. I wouldn't walk out on him and never abandon him.

Do I fear Rich? Yes sometimes I think he will find me. But than I remind myself he wouldn't bother. Other times I don't sleep nights thinking that he would bother because I took away his son, and even though he doesn't care, it would piss him off. I've done everything I could to ensure my safety and my son's safety in spite of it and I am in a good place now. I took him back every time, but never again. He is a part of my past and without him I would not have my precious child. So no regrets on my end. I got the best of the best out of a bad situation. I couldn't be more blessed.

He didn't deserve me, and I know that now. But sometimes it takes someone to really show you that, and he did. I carry a lot of the scars he put on me, hell half my face is paralyzed! I see this everyday but for that reason I fight hard and win every battle I enter.

You can bruise the body, mind and spirit, but a child closes wounds you never knew you had and gives you the love that you unconditionally deserve. I will always cherish our good times and not think of the bad ones. But even now all memory of him is starting to fade. Time truly does heal all wounds, you have to be willing to let it. Took me a long time to get to that point.

The Realization

So now here I am back in Rockland County, New York, where not a thing has changed and only a dime full of the people have. I keep asking myself why I came back, and eventually I'll have an answer. I had a few at the time I moved, but they are fading fast as I go along.

The initial reasoning being I wanted my son to have roots. And because mine were here, I thought that would be a good starting place. But I'm questioning that as well. As much as things are the same, the things that have changed, have not been for the better. And my name still has stayed the "Alicia Genna" from the past. The "crazy" girl who's family was off-balance and always in the papers. And hey, who knows maybe I am, but who really cares? I love who I am, what I am and what I have become. I have confidence and no fears. So maybe being crazy is better than being "normal" or even average. Who knows!

As insane as it is, it has honor in it; the fact that people have not forgotten me and that I left an impression. Most people, if they leave somewhere they are remembered for a while, but than they are forgotten. Ten years and I still am speaking to the same people and more who remember me from middle school.

God Bless.

It's not just what it is, It's what you make it.

My Mission

What I hope to provide is some guidance. I never accepted the term: "been there, done that," so I say in my own way , I have seen and been through a great many things. I would like to explain the best I can on the why and how I got through. I would also like to give you an idea as to how I think and give all subjects my own edge.

I gave you a brief auto-biography to let you know that no one is perfect and that we are all with flaws, scars and hurts No matter what, we still have the power of our stories. My father for example chose to write "the end" where I on the other hand choose to write "to be continued." We choose our path, We decide our destination, and We make the final decision.

As I share as much as I can with you, I hope you have an open mind and open heart, for this will go from one end of the spectrum to the other. All based on opinions. What facts I give are always quoted, but the idea is that I am just human, and with that I want to give hope so that when faced with scenarios, you are now with more options. Our teachers always taught us to be prepared right? This isn't that different.

I have been writing most of my life, not to help myself, but to help others to get through, or to avoid what I didn't, or couldn't. I have wondered many times why I was chosen to get all these obstacles on my road, and what I learned is, I am here to enlighten and help others. I'm not a prophet, don't get me wrong, but I am here for a reason. We all are and never forget that.

And with that, everything will be okay. Just Believe.

Just Because.

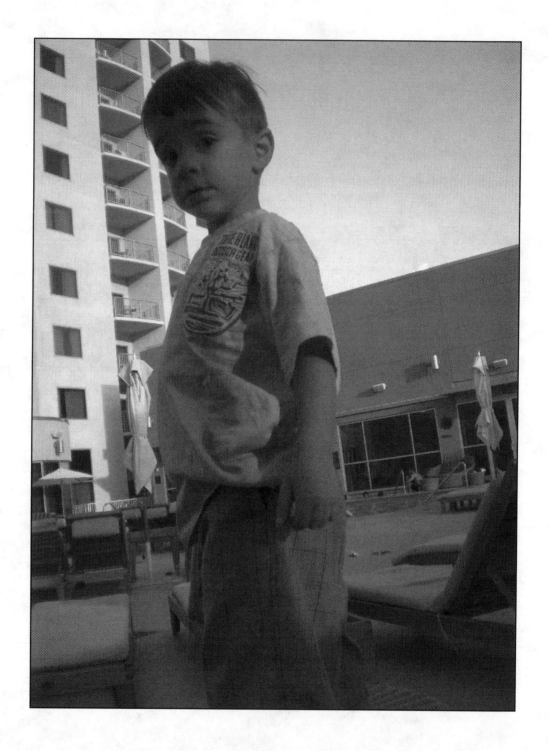

A child...Unconditional...

Should I go with how much a child is a blessing? Should I say how much mine is not only a blessing but the meaning of life and what makes me whole? Should I say that not only is my child happy, but he is healthy and spoiled.

The wrath of a mother angry for her child is a fear to be recognized. I've only been a mother for four years, but it feels like forever and that feeling, is indescribable. Point being there a few things I picked up on the way.

A mother will do anything for her child. She will fight, love, care, coddle even kill for her child. Its a bond that no other individual would understand. You've seen mothers in animals, there's no difference in the human realm of it. We mothers create and bond with our child during pregnancy and just gets stronger day in and day out. It's not something taken for granted and its not something to be used in any negative way. I've seen unfit parents and I've seen mothers use children as excuses.

I've had the experience of my mother not wanting me, but she still clawed out when necessary which tells me that the unconditional is forever whether you want it or not. The other thing is that its out Greatest weakness. It can and will be used against us many times, but to recognize and understand that, it should be okay for you to deal with.

People are vicious creatures. Know your weakness and know that your child will be used as one of them, next being family. But remember as I have said before, The two things that stem from it being one: the jealousy and Two: them KNOWING that it will or Can bring you down to your knees if you let it. if you sink to that level you will suffer. but if you believe and know and have than you should have nothing to worry about. And if your child is more special than others like mine, remember that the first thing to be said is illness. Be strong, Believe, and Have faith.

Let God have his way with those who need it. He's far more powerful than we can ever be and I would never want to be in his wrath just like I would never mess with a mother and her child. When you see your child smiling all the time, you should never question anything else because not only do you know best.. you feel what they feel.

Let me shed some light (Schizophrenia)

I would like to share something a bit different on something I believe to be important. I've heard this "label" tossed around one to many times, and I don't believe it should be used so lightly.

Unless you have met and socialized with a schizophrenic than you will know that not only is the disease itself not something to joke about, but how hard it is for that person to take on a daily living and most don't make it. they quit earlier than their time by God and leave the pain behind. But here's what I don't want to do ,and that's summarize what schizophrenia is because you can Google it yourself and most of us think we know what it is anyway. What I would like to do is help you understand that before you go around the name as a harmless insult, let me give you a behind the scenes look at what kind of insult your hurling out...

I want you to do something first. I want you to know who you are for a second. just completely and realize that right now you know that you are who you are and are doing what you are doing. now like a flash of light imagine being gone. like a black out but worse. Imagine having your body keep going , but your mind not there with it. than, like a flash of light all of a sudden your back, but you have no recollection of what happened and no idea what was done or how long you were not coherent. At the same time you know that you weren't there, you know "you were". That is Multiple Personality Disorder and has nothing to do with schizophrenia.

Its when post traumatic stress disorder isn't enough and turns into something more unique for the mind to cope with situations, most common: abuse. And the example I just gave is what its like for someone to have that disorder whether its one other or 16 other personalities the idea is exactly the same. one personality is a "leader" but when there is more than one it usually stems from each one having a role to deal with "something" the person them self could not. such as anger, sadness, love, and so on. Its a very hard life and is curable so to speak, with medication and proper therapy, but imagine living like that on a daily basis and actually having that disease.

Schizophrenia is a funny disorder to me because in every scientific definition it really has no meaning other than a person being more paranoid, nervous and distressed more than the average. When studying this it led me to believe that in order to get another drug out it meant coming up with another name for a disorder for the brain. There is very much bad information out there about schizophrenia.

Some still believe it is like "Dr. Jekyll and Mr. Hyde." That is far from accurate. Especially since the Personality disorder came along it turned this disease into having several more meanings which in my head.. mean nothing more than that average person having things intensified by 10. So what is accurate on it? Honestly we won't ever know. for all we know my theory could be right in its nature and have no meaning at all. In Greek it stands for "the dividing of minds" but in all definitions it makes you understand that it has nothing to do with that. so it tends to be a contradicted disease.

Multiple personality disorder did not come to light (belief wise) until around 1992 and the reason being it was founded by a woman. Nobody believed her even as she treated her patient till the day she died, it still was not recognized until the patient died and her works of art showed her hands had been able to draw in many different ways (forms) in which ONE human would not be able to do as an individual. interesting theory isn't it.. No one believed because of how often people lie and due to the theory of "boy cried wolf" this was referred to as non-existent. Also the theory of Hysteria was big in the 60's leading through until this came onto the books. It was believed that when a woman was too stressed or could not behave or act normally she had Mass Hysteria and that was that. The meaning being too many hormones in easy terms... lovely isn't it... I do believe that if a Man were to have had this particular case, that this diagnosis would've came into the lime light a lot sooner. Even if the patient was male it would have been made a diagnosis sooner but of course being both the Therapist and Patient females, the whole thing was thought to be made up by the therapist to bring herself into fame. There so much on all this I could go on about but let me bring it home and to the point.

When someone calls someone schizophrenic and gives you a Google definition of the word itself and not really of how it pertains to them, understand that if you can do something, you tell them they are wrong or out of line, you are stepping up to a plate that not many can. You think of all those out there who suffer from different problems, but all in all its just known as "crazy" right? but here's my idea.. these "crazy people have to live in a harsh reality where their life everyday is a harder challenge than anyone can imagine and no pill can take that away unfortunately, only blur out what they are experiencing (hence "zombie mode") so does that make them crazy, or does that make them honorable and strong people for not falling off the horse and getting up everyday to still have a go at it.

I think that makes us crazy and them the strong ones we should learn from.

Like I said I can give you all sorts of definitions on schizophrenia but I won't because you have a brain and eyes, use it if you really want the book terms. in life terms, its basically just this; One person who has to take challenges harder than others, sees things slightly different depending on the degree of their diagnosis and paranoid because of how people treat them (do you blame them though)? Also Its a human with the same brain as you and me who just decides to work a little differently, sometimes faster, sometimes slower on different things areas. here is your classic book definition right out of my text: "The Schizophrenic disorder is thought to mainly affect cognition, but it also usually contributes to chronic problems with behavior and emotion. People with schizophrenia are likely to have additional (co morbid) conditions, including major depression and anxiety disorders;[7] the lifetime occurrence of substance abuse is around 40%. Social problems, such as long-term unemployment, poverty and homelessness, are common. Furthermore, the average life expectancy of people with the disorder is 10 to 12 years less than those without, due to increased physical health problems and a higher suicide rate (about 5%). So tell me, doesn't that sounds like 70% of the population.... and wouldn't that mean that you might be schizophrenic and not know it... but to be that, well it's just "crazy" right which is not acceptable anywhere so God Forbid!!!

Point is: know your facts and who your using them against. you want to do text book psychiatry work that's fine but don't discredit someone else because you don't know them and you are not happy that they are more successful than you. Also know what your using as a term before throwing it out as an insult to someone, because really the only person your hurting is yourself and making a disease that really has no president into something that it isn't.

Next time learn another word besides "crazy" and if you do use crazy.. have a definition behind it because in Sincere fact 99% of the population of the United States has "crazy" tendencies. so meaning? were all crazy in our own way now aren't we.

Wisdom over Words

Remember at one time when people would say something offensive, we would fly off the chain? At times when we got angry we did what we could to make sure others suffered too? and what about when we were jealous? How far did we go to make that person we were jealous of wish they were non-existent? But than we grew up, well most of us did. And on that path of growing the realization that the battles we fought once upon a time were worthless and petty and how much we hurt people in the process. it just wasn't worth it, but it was youth and as long as we learned from it its OK. But that's when you have those who don't learn, who don't grow, expand and gain knowledge and continue on with their antics of always wanting to hurt others and make others feel horrible. But why? To have control, which we know is an illusion.. To gain power? To punish? To make them feel better about themselves? Or maybe just because boredom and no conscious mixed in the equation and they call it fun now. But to me that just makes you a sick person. Very sick and disgusting. And than to use tactics such as family to add in to their battle, well that's just incredibly stupid but also psychotic. To be able to use some one's family, kids etc as a tactic to make someone feel low is a sickness and not in the range of normality. to be able to think, let alone do it is not sane in any sense of the word. So here's where wisdom comes in. Know what battle your fighting, and know why your fighting it. what are you fighting for? what are the benefits, and are you hurting others in the process like them? is it worth the time, let alone the energy to do this battle? and is the outcome worth anything or are you just sinking to their level and using their strategy in the process.. This is where you put your knowledge and strength to the test. Its easy to fight, to use words and to make others feel bad. In fact its too easy and too childish. But how Hard is it to ignore, to walk away and to say its not worth it and/or my time. To realize the stupidity of it, the lies and the twisted minds behind it and say "you know what? in the end, what is this really proving?" I've always said to myself, if someone can go low, well that's easy, but would you want to join them? when you came so far and are now high, why take steps down that ladder for others, when you actually take a step up from using this as another learning notch on your belt. you just became that much smarter, wiser and stronger because you chose the adult thing, this wise move and the higher road. So in actuality who won the fight? that battle that wasn't worth your energy, when you walked away, you already won. you gained the power to be able to know the difference between right and wrong. sane and insane. and the major difference between having control """ and holding power. Control is not real so the people thinking they are controlling a situation or a fight really aren't doing anything are they? but the person holding on to their power, their strength and sanity for something better to fight for, well they just redeemed more points for realizing some things, just aren't worth fighting. We all know we won't always win every battle we are in. But if we tried and it was worth the effort than that should be good enough. Sometimes we need to learn to let God take some of it too. We can't always face everything alone. Give it all you got, but if you do and you still need more, put your faith to test. That's how I realized how powerful God can be and how much he can do for us. If only we believe. I try to bring him to every ones life, and its not always excepted but that's OK. we all are different and have different opinions, views etc. There is absolutely nothing wrong with that, and that's usually where people end up having words over. its not worth it. everyone is entitled to their own " to each their own" and if its not accepted than hey, their not good enough. Know your strengths and your weaknesses. I will promise you this, and I would know best, Nobody will know how strong you are as an individual and of mind, but everyone will know your weaknesses and use them against you. if you know both than you will recognize when to use the strength and when to ignore those who use the weaknesses as a vice. As for me, I know both and use both when needed, recognize both when used and understand to a full capacity. Like I said, it's so easy to join a fight and kick up a defense, but so hard to walk the other way knowing you already won and sit back and wait. I've been through so much to sum it up. I have said before, if you can walk in my shoes for a day, maybe I will care to listen for a minute, until than all I see or hear is a buzz when things turn to the worst. If anyone thinks words are going to break me, words of insanity, words of nonsense and lies and the use of my family in false truths,,, than they have so much to learn. I have full body armor which is good and bad. Good for things like this as I just endured a group with all this recently and a battle I chose to win, but bad because I have many walls up. meaning when that one person comes alone, if the walls don't just fall, there's going to be a lot of hammering! But that's OK. I'm strong, I'm wise and I'm powerful. I have a beautiful son, caring friends and a wonderful family even with its faults. I have nothing to hide and will use all I have endured and continue to endure to help others. God Bless and remember, be you, nothing else is good enough to try on. ~A. Sometimes its worth it to let people think they have won... That way they learn the hard way because no one comes out of a fight without a scratch, and if it wasn't you..... Some say Karma, I say its you that holds that power in such situations. Use it wisely.

Lies, or Truths..

When Reality sets in, we tend to see things that we never wanted to see from the beginning. The question is, what are we going to do about it? So were always faced with decision making, and we always choose our own path, yet we have this tendency to blame others for our failings. Even petty things we use another as an excuse as to the "why".

Is it nature or nurture?

My idea, is that its neither. were accustomed to doing things the way we want them done. when something is out of it's natural order, as we see it, we tend to rebel in our own way. Whether its blaming, or using excuses it doesn't matter the fact is we all are liars. I can't tell you how many times I have heard someone say I never lie, or I suck at lying. or what about the old, I don't lie, I stretch the truth. first of all let me point out to you if you had the nerve to say you don't lie, you just lied not only to the person you told but to yourself because we all lie. whether its a petty white lie, a huge lie or a life saving lie, you have lied. That's not always a bad thing. but if you can't recognize yourself for doing it, that's when you usually become pathological about it.

I know so many who tell more lie than truths. I can actually say that they lie so much the truth doesn't exist no more to them. they actually believe what they tell. does that mean their not lying? no that would be an excuse. it just means that if you feel the need to lie that much, you lose yourself at some point in time. so is it worth it? and getting caught.. is that worth it? we all have this notion that "we'll never get caught" but statistics show opposite. I believe that most of us would believe them to be super-natural if they could and tell everyone so... Its just amazing because, what happens when your with that someone special and now realize you don't want to lie anymore? do you understand that in order for that to happen you have to tell the person you are a liar. that you have to retrain yourself to be able to tell the truth. Do you understand that the person trusting you is very slim, but this is because how would they know whether your being honest about changing..? There are so many factors that we never look at let alone consider in this life. we see things as a day to day. I know the people who are planners, will say "yeah a year from now..." but in all actuality those are the ones who are more day to day then the next.. why? well because how can you make that one thing come true and prevent it from being a lie unless you make everyday come out exactly right to live up to what its going to be like "a year from now." Never thought about that I bet... so what about us honest ones who are told so often "I don't lie" and we just sit there and believe it.

we do so because we hope that this one, this time will be different and maybe they really don't lie. but its so hard because in all essence, we never really believe anything they say anyway.. do we? so how do you know if your a liar or an honest one? Do you go around telling people you don't lie? that's your first wrong. Do you lie about small things thinking its Okay because its a white lie? that's your second notion. Would you lie in a situation to get yourself out of it, or make yourself look OK, better or not involved? I'll tell you real quick. if you answered yes to any of these there's a good chance that you lie but your not pathological about it. if you answered no to any or all of these your a pathological liar. your so far gone you actually believe your own lies. Its sad but that's life isn't it? we get to pick out who our "crowd" is. just know that it defines you in every way. you have one friend who's a liar, one who's a cheat one who steals and one who says their "different" you have one screwed up situation. And the worst one in that group.. the "different" one. of course right! How far would you go to make someone believe something? How far would you go to make yourself believe something? How far would you go till you realize how far gone you are? would you even get to the point of realization? or would you live your whole life a lie?

Identity...

Sometimes who we think we are, we are really not. When you are not real, or true to yourself, it becomes so natural that you lose your sense of self and identity. But how far are you willing to go.. And why care what others think of you? Some strive so hard to be someone there not. Some even try to be someone they know, just to be accepted. People go to great lengths to be what I call a people pleaser. But in the end who are you really pleasing? I never understood that whole concept of thinking but I can understand why people are driven to think like that. Meaning.. Our society is based so matter of fact on certain issues, if you do not live up to "what is expected" you are not normal. And that brings us back to the label theory.. but with all that's going on, will people never learn that its about making yourself happy not others. your the one who goes to sleep at night and wakes up in the morning. your tactics and priorities need to be altered...

The lengths of Beauty....

It's amazing what we women do for beauty. We go to such lengths to succeed in anything other than natural beauty. but why? what is the sole purpose of it? does it bring gratification to the woman herself, or is it to bring gratification for a man? We all have our secrets and our tricks of the trade so to speak. some still shave, while others get waxed. than we have epilators and lasers to "permanently" remove hair. and what about make up. there's always new looks coming out, with new colors. how can you even keep up with the trends? and you never achieve the look you saw to begin with, so you usually end up back with what you were using. not to mention we have "permanent" make up. but the question for that is, what happens when you get sick of that particular look? you can't just wipe it off. And do we realize and understand that "models" on covers or in magazines do not look like that in real life. Between air brushing and photo shop they literally create an image from a person. that person does not exist though, which is what leads us to disappointment when that look can't be achieved..

Hair, well I can say personally that I do it for change. I like to see reactions from others, but mostly I like the way hair defines a face. Its amazing what someone looks like with one color, change it and you can create a new face. But some do it for the wrong reasons all together. As a stylist we are very close to the therapist business. we hear and see things that they wouldn't even dare tell their therapists even. Usually its break-ups. for those with the long hair they want it gone and those with short want it long. so extensions come in the picture now. Than our light haired gals want to go dark, and our dark want to go light. It's always a dramatic change, where what it should be is subtle leading into... But in extreme situations, we tend to do extreme things. A way to tell a good stylist from a bad one; very simple. depending on your hair, go in and tell him/her you want to go with a drastic change. if they say nothing or anything but "why" or "what's going on", you know they are not good. A good one does not go and do what you want at that second, but tries to find out the why first, so you don't walk out in tears with your money in their pocket. A Real stylist should care enough to sometimes send someone away if they feel the decision a person wants will lead them into something bad, or into something they will not like. I have done so before and also been thanked for it.

Plastic surgery. the numbers on this is astronomical and change everyday so me listing them is a waste of time. these surgeons are living it up I can definitely say that much. I have yet to see or hear of one that does not drive a hummer h2; which I find weird. But all these changes we make to our bodies, what we don't realize is that nothing is permanent. When was the last time someone really was told the truth about breast implants? for example, did you know that the maximum life of them is 10 years. or what about the leakage factor is higher than 60% and does go through your system (why they changed it to saline). and that they can and will pop at one time or another which is not only painful, but than requires extensive surgery (money) with recovery time, a new implant (money), with more recovery time. the recovery times are not small either. they go from 6-12 weeks! liposuction runs from 4-8 weeks! a tummy tuck can go from 3-6 months with results not seen for 2 years. But are people being told all this? how much information do we really know on all these topics?

Permanent ink, tattoos. I myself have over a dozen but I know all the effects caused from them. but how many artists know? they don't go to school, they apprentice with an existing artist. watch and learn and go on their own. how safe do you feel really? also the whole needle factor. I hate looking but I make sure that package is brand new. the machine itself, did you know has to be replaced every 6-9 months or screw ups occur. and ink does go bad, but how often do they replace their ink and how would we know? Those are just some things, but when placed on your body here's some thoughts for you. did you know that everyday the ink sinks further and further into your skin (why fading occurs). our skin replenishes and sheds ever 24-48 hours depending on age. its got to go somewhere. when there's no skin left, it seeps through the tissue and now into your blood stream. have you ever read or has your stylist ever told you that hair color can result different for those with tattoos? It's something you should be asked. there is now metallic's in your blood. they effect the body in many ways. and when you get a prescription, there is a label for that as well, but when have you heard a doctor say, "do you have tattoos?" Everything is so rush lately that the little things we think are minor are actually very serious. We put things to the side because one person doesn't say it, so well than who needs to know right? Well I think before women do any kind of procedure, even men, ask questions. research first. this include nails. we've heard of people getting diseases and bacterial infections due to improper cleaning and disinfecting. But what about acrylics? do you know what grows under them on your nails after just a week.

know who is doing what to you and make sure he/she has all the right licensing and certification. it costs millions to live, but nothing to die.

Understand, Accept than proceed..

To understand others, you have to fully understand yourself, who you are as a whole, accept it and than proceed. As long as it took me, and the frustrations it gave me, I finally made it to that point and I will proceed to share with you what I have learned.

We all should know where we stem from, where our roots begin and spread to and from, and who is our guardians through our life. Those that keep us planted on the ground and able to walk that extra mile even when were ready to hit the pavement... We should also give thanks every day for our many blessings and stop forgetting we have them. Not everyone is so fortunate. Open your eyes and look up; see what you forgot along the way and Give Thanks now, To God for the ability to stand let alone see, when in fact you never know the day you may not be able to do neither...

I might be walking along side you on path and see everything that's going on, where you might only have seen the couple on the opposite path and maybe someone walking their dog. But I always wonder why "you" didn't see that there were 4 kids in the yard on the other side of the street and a teenager waking the opposite direction of us, while an old lady was sitting on her front porch and some man was tending to his garden.. I believe it is just a gift, or maybe an ability for me to see as well as feel all the energy that buzzes around me. I am able to not miss anything and see things others don't notice, or maybe just don't want to.. you have to learn to let things go when they are not working good for you anymore.

This was the hardest for me to do, and still to this day is the hardest sometimes for me to work on. Letting things go used to be so near impossible for me. I used to build it like mounds on my shoulders until I would just snap one day with frustration and anger. But even then you do not release anything but your own negative energy stored on your body. Whether it be food, products, or people and situations, they should never be allowed in your life or to stay in your life if no good.

Anything that is overwhelming to you should never be in your path. if it is too much and not worth a grain of salt, throw it over your shoulder and be on your way. take it off your back and keep walking.. "End is a natural thing, every end is a new beginning. Nothing new can start without letting the old go."

As easily angered as I am, it comes from a reason or source. Anger is usually provoked. I have worked on it though. I will say I have been able to maintain a clean wall for quite a long time now. Anger is never real as some might think. Its not an emotion but simply a feeling to cover an emotion not wanting to be felt, such as sadness. I believe that we get angry to easily these days because we are truly afraid to show emotions for thoughts of what people might think. But when you get angry, don't people think anyway? Don't they talk just the same? So is it worth it and what was the point?... The way I feel is we should be surrounded by positive energy at all times. If there is negative, step out of that dark light and enter a new one. Nobody has the Right to disrupt a natural order of 'what should be.' It is said that I am easily jealous; yet with everything and everyone in my life I have no reason to doubt anything. The trust and bond I have with the people in my life are tight enough not to question or think otherwise. Jealousy too is not worth an emotion or a feeling because it is usually brought on by talk of others, who are ironically... jealous. Know what you have and if it feels wrong to where jealousy enters the picture, believe it to be negative and leave it be.

"Observant, Careful and cautious, thinks quickly with Independent thoughts." I have led an independent life from age 11 until now. I've always been the observant type. I could sit and people watch for hours. It's fascinating to me because I can tell you who's thinking what, who wants what, who is fake/ who is real, what their real thoughts are when they speak - and what they don't want people to hear. That's where the careful and cautious come in. sometimes I speak to quickly because of that and shout people out so to speak. I have learned to think quicker before speaking and now am able to give you straight face; but not only do I know the truth, I laugh at you without you having any idea.

"Loves to lead." I believe that to lead is to learn as well as to guide. If your leading your going to see and experience first, which means you have to learn. you are not born with the ability to climb, you learn it, so for example if I run into a wall, in order to lead a pack, I have to learn to climb and than guide the others as to the how to as well. I've never once followed for many reasons, and that ranges from it being boring, to losing a sense of self and never building character. I call it fence sitting. If you are a fence sitter you watch others go by and you go no where. its the same if you follow all the time. how can you make yourself into just "you" if you have followed in others footsteps... you have nothing to speak of yourself, but only of others and their accomplishments. I want my footprints in the sand to stand out and be the first pair you see, don't you?

"protective are you over others who you have accepted into your life, you will fight for them and god help the one who dared to try and harm your loved ones." How often am I a lover, but when crossed or I feel a loved one being crossed will I leap. That is big to me. no one should ever have to suffer what they need not to suffer, and if I am able to prevent that, I will in any means possible. I have The bear who is here to remind me that not every situation calls for a violent response. Violence is never a solution to a problem. it gets you no where in the end. I just never understood in the first place, nor will I ever, why people want to hurt others mentally or physically. What's the point? To make yourself feel better in the process? Are you that inept and blind that you use others to make yourself feel good? And even than, could you not have found a different way?.... Does it feel good to see one hurt and/or cry, and know you were the reason why...If so their is a mental instability you must overcome. So in the end it will ultimately be you crying and hurt. Whatever happened to: "Do unto others as you would have done to you "Did that get lost along the way? If so, don't you believe your going down the wrong path...

Natural Order"

"Life is not measure by the number of breaths we take but by the moments that Take Our Breath Away..."

Two Choices: What would you do?....you make the choice. Don't look for a punch line, there isn't one. Read it anyway. My question is: Would you have made the same choice?

At a fundraising dinner for a school that serves children with learning disabilities, the father of one of the students delivered a speech that would never be forgotten by all who attended. After extolling the school and its dedicated staff, he offered a question: 'When not interfered with by outside influences, everything nature does, is done with perfection. Yet my son, cannot learn things as other children do. He cannot understand things as other children do. Where is the natural order of things in my son?' The audience was stilled by the query. The father continued. 'I believe that when a child like him, who was mentally and physically disabled comes into the world, an opportunity to realize true human nature presents itself, and it comes in the way other people treat that child.' Then he told the following story:

"My son and I had walked past a park where some boys he knew were playing baseball. He asked, 'Do you think they'll let me play?' I knew that most of the boys would not want someone like him on their team, but as a father I also understood that if my son were allowed to play, it would give him a much-needed sense of belonging and some confidence to be accepted by others in spite of his handicaps. I approached one of the boys on the field and asked (not expecting much) if he could play. The boy looked around for guidance and said, 'We're losing by six runs and the game is in the eighth inning. I guess he can be on our team and we'll try to put him in to bat in the ninth inning.' My son struggled over to the team's bench and, with a broad smile, put on a team shirt. I watched with a small tear in my eye and warmth in my heart. The boys saw my joy at my son being accepted. In the bottom of the eighth inning, his team scored a few runs but was still behind by three. In the top of the ninth inning, my son put on a glove and played in the right field. Even though no hits came his way, he was obviously ecstatic just to be in the game and on the field, grinning from ear to ear as I waved to him from the stands. In the bottom of the ninth inning, his team scored again. Now, with two outs and the bases loaded, the potential winning run was on base and my son was scheduled to be next at bat. At this juncture, they let him bat and gave away their chance to win the game. Everyone knew that a hit was all but impossible because he didn't even know how to hold the bat properly, much less connect with the ball. However, as he stepped up to the plate, the pitcher, recognizing that the other team was putting winning aside for this moment, moved in a few steps to lob the ball in softly so my son could at least make contact. The first pitch came and he swung clumsily and missed. The pitcher again took a few steps forward to toss the ball softly. As the pitch came in, he swung at the ball and hit a slow ground ball right back to the pitcher. The game would now be over.

The pitcher picked up the soft grounder and could have easily thrown the ball to the first baseman. my son would have been out and that would have been the end of the game. Instead, the pitcher threw the ball right over the first baseman's head, out of reach of all team mates. Everyone from the stands and both teams started yelling, ' run to first! Run to first!' Never in his life had my son ever run that far, but he made it to first base. He scampered down the baseline, wide-eyed and startled. Everyone yelled, 'Run to second, run to second!' Catching his breath, he awkwardly ran towards second, gleaming and struggling to make it to the base. By the time he rounded towards second base, the right fielder had the ball . the smallest guy on their team who now had his first chance to be the hero for his team. He could have thrown the ball to the second-baseman for the tag, but he understood the pitcher's intentions so he, too, intentionally threw the ball high and far over the third-baseman's head. My son ran toward third base deliriously as the runners ahead of him circled the bases toward home. All were screaming, his name.as he reached third base because the opposing shortstop ran to help him by turning him in the direction of third base, and shouted, 'Run to third! run to third!' As he rounded third, the boys from both teams, and the spectators, were on their feet screaming, ', run home! Run home!' he ran to home, stepped on the plate, and was cheered as the hero who hit the grand slam and won the game for his team 'That day', said the father softly with tears now rolling down his face, 'the boys from both teams helped bring a piece of true love and humanity into this world'.

My son didn't make it to another summer. He died that winter, having never forgotten being the hero and making me so happy, and coming home and seeing his Mother tearfully embrace her little hero of the day !

Now isn't that how nature should be, and how we should naturally teach our children to be?

Doubts.. Why me..

Sometimes we wonder, 'What did I do to deserve this?' or 'Why did God have to do this to me?' BUT...What if it's really all just so simple, and were blindsided by what is, rather than what could be... So here's a story. Use it in any way you would like.

A daughter is telling her Mother how everything is going wrong, she's failing algebra, her boyfriend broke up with her and her best friend is moving away. Meanwhile, her Mother is baking a cake and asks her daughter if she would like a snack, and the daughter says, 'Absolutely Mom, I love your cake.' 'Here, have some cooking oil,' her Mother offers. 'Yuck' says her daughter. 'How about a couple raw eggs?' 'Gross, Mom!' 'Would you like some flour then? Or maybe baking soda?' 'Mom, those are all yucky!' To which the mother replies: 'Yes, all those things seem bad all by themselves. But when they are put together in the right way, they make a wonderfully delicious cake!' God works the same way. Many times we wonder why He would let us go through such bad and difficult times. But God knows that when He puts these things all in His order, they always work for good! We just have to trust Him and eventually, they will all make something wonderful!

Remember BELIEVE. "God would not give us something we could not handle." He gives us what we need in order to grow and build strength. God is crazy about you. He sends you flowers every spring, a sunrise every morning and a sun set every evening. Whenever you want to talk, He'll listen. He can live anywhere in the universe, and He chose your heart.

"Life may not be the party we hoped for, but while we are here we might as well dance!" So when you have doubts, don't understand and wonder why?.. Look at the Whole picture and not just the pieces crumbling; sometimes those pieces are just in the way for a smoother layer of frosting!

Exposure.. What is AS?

"Children with AS (Aspergers Syndrome) learn to talk at the usual age and often have above-average verbal skills. They have normal or above-normal intelligence, and the ability to take care of themselves. The distinguishing features of AS are problems with social interaction, particularly reciprocating and empathizing with the feelings of others; difficulties with nonverbal communication (e.g., facial expressions); peculiar speech habits that include repeated words or phrases and a flat, emotionless vocal tone; an apparent lack of "common sense"; a fascination with obscure or limited subjects (e.g., doorknobs, railroad schedules, astronomical data, etc.), often to the exclusion of other interests; clumsy and awkward physical movements; and odd or eccentric behaviors (hand wringing or finger flapping; swaying or other repetitive whole-body movements; watching spinning objects for long periods of time)."

"Although less is known about adults with Asperger syndrome, they are often described as having rigid interests, social insensitivity, and a limited capacity for empathizing with others. Many individuals are highly creative and excel in areas such as music, mathematics, and computer sciences. They tend to excel in fields that require little social interaction. AS appears to be much more common in boys. It's a close relative to Autism."

So now you have a run-down on how my child works. And to the parents out there, you can only imagine what its like for him. Forget me! its a bit frustrating for me time to time, but watching him and knowing he's being judged breaks my heart and makes me more tough on others when they speak of him in any negative way. I will stand for my child as long as I live. he is part of me and is everything in this world to me. But me, I'm just me. I'm a woman who's been there done that, and yeah I got stories to tell and I'm doing just that. Don't expect much from me though. I do what I can, when I can, but I'm no different from A, B or C out there.

Curve Ball..

Ever get a straight ball and catch it, than you turn around and get hit in the back with a curve ball? And you never saw it coming. I believe that the true meaning of life is to make peace, make happiness and make an identity. people fall short of one or more of the above because sometimes, its too hard. But when we look at what we are given, is it really hard, or are we just lazy creatures, or maybe even creatures of habit who expect things to be handed to us. It would be nice to have things done for us and those curves taken care of without lifting our own fingers to do so, but what would that make us? and would we be what we wanted to be, or just "another" someone out there without a name.

Only God knows how many curve balls have been thrown my way, and I can say two things about that. The first being I have caught some, and the other being that I never let it hit me too hard. I take it with a "grain of salt" and do what I have to in order to throw the ball back. But what about you? have you been thrown curves and let them just hit you and walk away? or have you tried to pick that ball up and get it moving again? How hard is it really to look and see what we need to do. Yes, some tasks are going to be hard and tiring but isn't that what makes it worth it? Don't you want to be able to say that you won that battle. Don't you want to take what you need to and make it your own so to speak. I know that without all that's been thrown my way, I would not be who I am today and not only do I pride myself on that but I am grateful for it. I wouldn't be able to sit here and write if I had nothing to say.. So why do I write.. Well for many reasons but I will break it down to simpler forms for you to understand. I started writing when I was 9 to be able to put the thoughts in my head into perspective. I had no one to talk to than nor do I really now, who's able to say "I completely understand." And honestly I wouldn't want that. Its what makes me, me. I am a talker and I am also an open book. I hide nothing because I believe I was put here to help others through their trials and stipulations and make sure they don't take the easy way out, or give up before they even tried. Everything I have been through and go through is not exactly a test to me. Some maybe, but most I believe to be a learning experience to speak of to others about. I see myself as a guide, not a follower and I know that my whole life I have been like that. At early ages I was guiding friends, family or even people I never knew just so they got to where they needed to be. I stop randomly and speak to people and we get into conversations that always lead to where I give advice before I walk away. Some find it annoying that I do so, others fascinated because I approach people without thinking or problem and start speaking.

I can tell you out of a line-up who needs guidance. I have that ability and I don't take that lightly. I also feel that people know that and they feel easy and relaxed talking to me. I meet a stranger and within 2 minutes know more about them than probably their best friend. And I didn't ask a question throughout the conversation. It just all comes naturally. Some people have to realize their gifts, because we all have one or more to share. there are healers out there that just their hands and touch have changed peoples lives. Doctors who went above and beyond to fight for causes they believed so strongly in. therapists who never give up on someone even if they choose not to work sync with them. Look around you and see how many people are out there doing something, even those you know who have stories to tell or things to give.

In each and every one of us there is something. What happens usually is we choose to not see it or ignore it. So when your faced with an issue, problem, situation, so on, are you going to pick up that ball and get it moving again, or are you going to just let it sit there and never know your own true potential? Think about it. everything should be for use it in a positive way.

A Lie... Or a Cover up..

What if everything you knew and believed turned out to be a lie... In 1998 my mother and I received a call informing us that my brother would be going to prison for 15 yrs. My mother was not shocked and I didn't know what to feel at that time because it seemed he was in jail more often than not. But what if you found out everything about that day, what had happened and to the day my brother "committed suicide" was a lie...

He didn't' deserve what outcome was handed to him. Before I proceed to tell you what I know now, let me know what I thought than. My brother was never suicidal. Never spoke of it, and I know would never take the easy way out. He had mentioned it once or twice to my mother but even than not convincing enough.

When I got the phone call,I was at my cousin's house with friends and we were just hanging out watching movies. My mom was the first to find out and called my Aunt and Uncle to tell them and to tell me. My older cousin took me in his kitchen looked at me and I freaked. I thought something had happened to my mom. He said no she was Okay, it was Cary. So I kept saying" WHAT; WHAT HAPPENED? "he hesitated, I wanted to kill him! Finally his voice broke and said "Ally, Cary's dead." I can't tell you what happened from there. I don't remember I blacked out. We were all to believe that he committed suicide in his cell that night on August 26, 2000. That he hung himself from the top bunk with his sheet, and threw his blanket over the bars so the guards would not know. I lived with that, my family lived with that, for years. For me though, for some reason than it haunted me because I knew something wasn't right.

My instincts were telling me I was missing something, and they were right.. And than one day I get a letter from a man I've never heard of or spoke with...

"Dear Alicia,

Cary always spoke so much of you. He said you were his sister and how much he loved you so I figured you were the best to contact. You don't know me and I don't really know you other than what I've heard but I'm confiding in you to tell you what really happened the night your brother died. Please don't blame me for waiting this long to do so, finding you was one thing, and hiding this so the guards wouldn't know was the other... The day your brother died, he was very anxious. Like he knew something was not right. your brother got me through some tough times in here and I want you to know he hung tough too. But that day was not the normal Cary. He was just released again from isolation which they kept him most of the time for one stupid thing or another. your brother always stood for himself, got in trouble for it, but he never backed down. know he was brave and never gave up who he was for nobody and to me that speaks in volumes. After he was released from isolation (solitary confinement) he was brought to lab to work with computers. He lit up a cigarette and the guards hassled him. all day they were on his ass for some reason. Finally later that night he didn't want to eat and they gave him a tough time about it. They started to beat him. but your brother always fought back. not smart, but he never backed down, I think mostly it was pride. Here's the thing, I saw your brother die, I saw how he died and I know why he died. The guards went to far. They took the beating to far this time and your brother hit his head hard when he went down face first from a crack in the back. He never moved after that. I think he died on impact, but the guards didn't stop there either. What I want you to know is that your brother did not commit suicide. he did not take the easy way. know that, because he would have suffered and endured a hell of a lot more. I know that. Please do not hate me and please don't seek me out. I was Cary's cell mate once a long time ago in Syracuse, just so happened this time we had cells next to each other. I believe it was meant that way for me to be able to tell you this. I loved your brother dearly and back than he even taught me to read. don't know how anyone couldn't love him. Only person I knew that ever gave a damn. take care and live well. "

Tito.

As much as that is word for word, his words were, not so with manner.. so I had to change some to be able to write this. All in all it's the point that counts.

I read it several times and than screamed. I had to seek out a lady who was very close friends with my brother who was at the funeral. Took me a couple days but I found her and we talked. She knew Tito and she read the letter. She already knew.

I remembered him after my father and that also clued me in that he wouldn't have the guts to do it. How did I know that. well lets get some facts on the table, before I went and got my own.

The guards sweep the floor so to speak every 3-5 minutes checking mates until lights out. Not to mention the camera's on each cell mate. My brother died before lights out. It was said a blanket was thrown over the bars of my brothers cell. If that were true than they would have been on him like white on rice. Whether or not the guards pay attention to the cameras, they do notice movements like that and its not allowed. That blanket would have alerted the staff and there goes that. You get the idea, the rest is for me to be at peace with.

At Cary's wake I saw the bruise on his forehead, looked down his shirt saw the bruises but no ring collar at his throat stating a hanging and his face was bruised as well. if I would've looked further I probably would uncover his body in bruises.

Sometimes instincts are enough. If you feel something is not right, or maybe that it is right, always follow your instinct. It may unveil a truth you needed to know.

True Love....

When you love, you love completely. You give yourself to them and accept them for who there are as a whole. You feel in love with them for that reason, if it should change you never loved at all. You should be able to trust them to the fullest and put your fears aside. And if some you can't than you face them head on as you would others. Always address what's needed to be talked about or understood and never leave the other guessing. When you love your heart is open, and its vulnerable, think about that and how easy it is to take advantage, and to hurt. So when you start questioning things does it mean that your not in love? and what about when you feel your trust is wavering, does it mean you don't trust, maybe never did? Do you find yourself questioning things that you didn't before and feel scared, confused and rushed? Welcome my friends, to the truest form and purest emotion of love. Nobody said it was easy. like life, its worth it though. The point of being with another is to build. "Rome was not built in a day" they say. But what can be built in a day? The idea is to lay a foundation. After you have that you start building on it. Nothing comes easy nor does it come quickly. Feelings have a way to make you feel rushed, even confused and lost sometimes. But in the end you must search your self for answers. Your heart.

The mind has a way of taking and receiving information, but it always plays tricks on us and I think we forget that sometimes and eventually start to believe it. That's why you seek your heart for confirmation. WE all have fears. We all have doubts and trust is not a normal subject. its very delicate, and if issues in the past where trust was shattered, or questioned, than expect it to be again. Your mind will do it to you, its inevitable. What you need to face is that because something happened before does not mean it will happen again. you have to use instincts rather than follow patterns.

Patterns always lead us backwards. We go through experiences to grow and learn from them, not to have them scar in us in a way that our present and future become affected. To gain or earn trust you must show trust. you must believe. remember just because you can't see something doesn't mean its not there or its not true. Sometimes it takes time though. Pushing someone aside is never the answer because our minds tend to take things to proportions where everything spins out of control. such as what ifs.. buts... how's... whys... and much more. but we know this, we have experienced this before.

I always say follow your heart in love because your heart is the first to hurt and last to heal, yet its the first to feel as well. if its able to feel, you trust it because it was the most affected. it will know what's right and wrong. it knows what you need and what you don't. It's a filter not only for the body but for the mind. Its our root of survival mental and physically. we forget that to often and lose so much that we don't need to lose and hurt ourselves and others in the process. To love you must be able to feel pain. To live you must be able to face fears. To do both you must be able to understand both and accept they come with each other. in every relationship there will be questions, there will be doubts, there will be fears and so on. What you need to realize is its a way for your mind to protect you from being hurt, but again, your mind is not always the smartest tool in every situation. sometimes we need to seek our hearts for the final destination. If your not willing to work, build and communicate you have nothing nor will you ever for these tools are not only for relationships but for everything you will go though we have all had our scares, we've all felt unwanted emotions, and we've all been under pressure. its what you do in the end that determines what kind of person you are. The cowards way is to always look the other way and walk. So ask yourself what type you are, and what would you do?

Comparisons

When I look at things I wonder how others see them compared to me. We all see things differently, but how differently, and is it an excuse? I know when I see someone down and out I do my best to try to help them in any way possible. I know also that they suffer because otherwise they wouldn't be that way. But why do other people choose to still be selfish and pretend as though they see nothing. Is it really that hard to take some time out of "your" life to help another, or are you that pretentious that all you think about is how glad that's not you, and go about your own way.

I understand what it feels like to be pushed aside, over seen, not taken seriously, put last and not helped in any way. Next time, instead of doing nothing, go out of your way to do something you would never normally do.

Simplicity....

Stop for a minute and let go of your need to rush every little thing. Simply enjoy the beauty that is right in front of you today.

You can look at a rose and see pure beauty and smell pleasure, or you can see thorns and prick your finger. either way the outcome is yours, so why not choose the better result...

Confusion...

When people say "I know how you feel" they usually say it for 3 reasons... empathy; being the least. sympathy; as runner up. Those who don't care or don't want to understand; your number one. We Are Selfish Creatures. Nature or Nurture... When was the last time you tried to put yourself in the position of someone else to the point where you can actually get a feeling of what's really going on? I can answer that for you, but you would call me a liar and I would call your bullshit... Nobody actually takes the time anymore to sit down, take a situation that someone is going through, put themselves in it, than feel what they would feel if that was actually them.

Now let me ask you again... when was the last time you put yourself in someone else's "shoes"? My bullshit call wasn't to far off the mark now was it... Its sad because I hear all the time just walking around and even personally someone say: "I feel you" or "I know how you feel" or how about "I can't imagine." That's my personal favorite. "I cant imagine." well if you can't imagine... don't act like you know, don't act like you care and don't say anything at all. When I say personal favorite I mean that in a sarcastic way; because to me if your that lazy, you can't take two seconds of Your time to "imagine" a situation that someone you care for is going through, you are a pretty horrible person.

its always those people that expect you to be there for them when shit hits the fan on their end... Expect you to not only just "imagine" but to care, have pity and put them on a pedestal. Pretty ironic if you ask me... so than you have those who are sympathetic. As a person, you are automatically sympathetic, so it can go two ways. you have those who say "oh I'm so sorry" and leave it at that because they do feel bad or what-not. But than you have those who either bring it to far with too many words just telling you they really don't care, and those who don't use any sympathy because they don't feel it. How many feelings and emotions do we not use because at that time you just didn't feel it; well sympathy is in the same category and some people don't use it at all. Than we have our empathetic individuals, and this is where it all gets mixed up. To be truly empathetic is to actually feel one's pain and suffering. They say God felt Jesus' pain and suffering at the time he was being nailed to the cross and that's why he took his soul. His body was a symbol of how the soul is what makes you the rest is just a shell. Now remember this is just opinions and thoughts. Now are you really empathetic? Don't get me wrong, some empathetic feel it in many different ways. I know some who will get horrible migraines over one's pain, some who get sick to their stomach, and those who feel it in their own heart. To be empathetic is to FEEL one's pain literally not figuratively.

I remember the lectures and debates over this, and how far some went to try to prove a point. In the end nobody could, it ended up back to whatever it was in the beginning. They say in Psychology that empathy comes from many different sources, such as one going through a similar experience, having a traumatic experience or even one just who is with the "gift" to feel. That one was always thrown off the table for the belief factor. Not many like to believe what they cannot see. But if you think about it, there are people out there who do have that gift, or as I put it, that curse to feel anther's pain.

So now we have all that established be careful what you say to someone because sometimes for one person, it could hurt more to hear bullshit out of one's mouth than to hear a simple "it's going to be OK," or "I will be here for you" and so on. What's the point in making a false statement? why make suffering more inevitable. For me, it's always been a mixture of all of the above. I'm not going to sit here an lie, there are times when I don't give a shit about someone's issues or problems, usually because they are petty and to me, not worth my time let alone theirs. but it's bad because to someone else, they really could believe that what they are dealing with is "the end of the world." Unfortunately because so many abuse it, it's become to close to "drama" and I don't listen to it. I wish I could say I always feel sympathetic, but for the reason I just described I can't. When a close friend or someone I love is going through a tough trial I do feel bad for them though. Do I feel it to the point of physical? no. I just Think to myself, that's horrible, and try to figure what I could do to help them at their time of need. This is not empathy but me being sympathetic and caring. But there are times when I do actually Feel someone's pain literally and not just in a figurative manner. Being empathetic has hit me more than once and this is when I started to believe it actually existed.

The first time I was too young to understand but when my father shot himself, I didn't know until the next day what really happened. meaning someone had to explain to me the events of what happened and that he was shot etc. But while his eyes were on me and the gun did fire, it felt as though my heart exploded. I can't even think of the words to describe it. there was so much pain and my body was so heavy. After I fled from the scene and hid and watched, I felt it slowly fade into nothing to the point of almost being free. at the time what I did not know, was what I was feeling was my father die. Being my first experience I would say it was a pretty crappy one. but I can actually say I know what my father felt at what moment and I know exactly when he slipped away. as scary as that sounds, I feel as though I shared the experience with him so he didn't have to be alone, and I know that he knew that as well. maybe it was meant to be that way. My father was the most empathetic person I've ever known, sometimes I wonder how he dealt with it. As I got older I felt things here and there but nothing to an extremity of me actually being concerned. Than my brother passed. The night my brother died I had pains in my ribs and horrible cramps. I figured, (sorry guy's), I was getting my time of the month, so I dealt with it. What scares me today is that, if he had "hung himself" as some believe or were led to believe, I know I would've felt that strangling and I don't know what that would have done to me... Another reason I know he didn't do what he was said to have done. but I've wrote on that before. What I felt it were where the marks I found on his body that day and another reason to make me check without consciously realizing it.

When I turned 18 the first thing I had done was hypnotism. what a joke I say. no matter what this Doctor did, I just sat there looking at him and it was funny. He told me I was just not ready yet. I told him he just sucked at what he does and laughed. so I hit the library and computer until I figured what out what I was looking for. I touched on this subject before, I found and learned EMDR.

When I had it done I realized that I did see some things that I didn't "remember" I blocked a lot more out than I realized. I did feel the things I felt (even though I refused to believe it) and learned why.

I was 19 yrs old and finding out that I had the ability to be empathetic. it scared the crap out of me. Who the hell wants to feel someone else's pain and suffering! At that point I was getting over my rebellious stage. I realized than I wanted out. I wanted out of Rockland County, of New York, out of the east coast all together. I needed to go somewhere that no one knew me and live a life freely. I ran away is more like it but that's Okay with me because I know that, accept it and wanted it. It benefited my needs as well. I was able to start over and learn who I was as a whole, go to college and learn everything I tried learning on my own. I was able to make friends that had nothing to base me on from the past, just who I really was and there is no greater feeling.

Here an there a friend or my ex-husband would go through something and I would feel it, but I came to accept the fact that I am able to feel. And that's all it is. It's feeling and a deeper understanding of what one is going through at that very moment. which is why I can and will call bullshit....

So your probably wondering where I'm going with all this. Well I had some ask me why I cared so much about others when I don't know them, don't like them, or when I can walk away and be Okay. Well it's pretty basic for me. Nothing and nobody in this world should have to feel like they're alone. I sit, or lie in bed at night and feel that way sometimes myself and my purpose I feel is to bring awareness to those who don't understand that we are not and never will be alone. There are so many things surrounding us, just because the human eye can't see it, doesn't mean it's not there. If angels were seen, would they be an angel? and wouldn't they be judged for having wings while "the normal" didn't. And what about our spiritual animal. Everyone of us has felt it in us at one point in our lives. and most likely will again. My spiritual animal being the Bear, with its instincts and strength; and my spiritual guide, the tiger with it being cunning and powerful (the warrior). I have felt that come out of me more than once. The night I was able to stand up to my ex I felt both my guides in me and it was amazing. It could go both ways though, so don't go looking for a fight... our guides our to direct us and help us through, but we choose our own battles. make sure you know just what your battling and know whether or not its worth it. "use your basic instinct."

Being alone physically can be a down turn for some. It does hurt to be alone. my description of me feeling alone, is my heart aches. not heart burn feeling, it just feels hollow. like an ache of wanting. Sometimes we even know someone's with us for example; a lost family member, but sometimes it still feels empty and that's normal. whatever "normal" might be. It's just a point where we need to learn how to get through what we need to on our own two and stop leaning for support. I would rather be alone than hear someone say "I can't imagine." and honestly, I can't stand sympathy it makes me sick. I'm no less of what I was, so don't look at me as if I weren't. Empathy, if you can't actually feel my pain, don't say you can. period. That's just me. We are all different. I'm more for hearing support and encouragement than "I can't even imagine...." So now think next time your going through something, an experience, trial, suffering, make sure you know what response you want before you speak. What I mean is, if you want sympathy make sure you know who your talking to. If you want someone to feel what your feeling than find an empathetic person to lean on. we are out there trust me. And if you want a liar, well you don't have to look to far sometimes, which is sad. Point is don't ask someone to feel what you feel unless they are able to. and if they are, than know they do understand to the fullest. if they can't, understand and don't expect anything more.

you can't make someone feel what you feel. its impossible. Even me, I've had some test me and see if I can just feel what they were feeling, I can't do that. its not a command or request that is available, it just is what it is. if not, know there's a deep understanding though. Sympathy is usually best from a loved one to just have them support you, not feel what you are going through. You build strength from it, always remember that. I myself expect some to step into my shoes and just feel what I feel sometimes, but than I remember.... God made us all different shoe sizes... Don't be what your not. Don't act one way when you feel another. Don't say things you don't know or mean. Don't tell someone to be something or someone they are not. Why lie, why cheat, why deceive, why hurt. What happened to caring, love, and being someone to depend on. That's what I'm here trying to do. Help make others understand, make them open their eyes and hopefully wake them up because we have so much of the other bullshit in this life. A little caring here and there makes a huge difference. For those who thought they were one thing and know they are not, you are no less of what you were. your the same, you just have a better understanding as to what is happening in situations and what you feel. I'd rather know than live a lie. People don't want lies and if they do they live in one. Do what you can and it should be enough. If not it's not your loss, now is it... you are able to walk away saying "I tried."

Something to think about...

They say an angel starts out with black wings. In order to achieve white they must prove themselves to be worthy... When we are born, we are born with innocence that no one really understands. A baby as well as a toddler is known to know nothing but. As we grow we adapt and become exposed to what's around us, we filter good from bad from what's around us. Either way we make choices on the way. Nobody can say they were wrong, because then you wouldn't be who you are today, now. Nobody can say they were right because you don't know the alternate option of what could have been. So in all actuality, I really don't think there is a right or wrong.

We feel our way through life with the wisdom we own and follow a path that was already set up for us. who's to say whether or not your on it, or if you strayed. You have so many opinions out there, for example the argument between nature vs. nurture, and what about the existence of earth and life. Some believe it was God, some say it was nature, and other countless opinions based off nothing. but who's to say their wrong. who's to say they are right. what we think is evil, how do we know it's evil vs. what we think is pure. Do we base things on what we learn or is it all personal? Get into an argument on ideas of a topic, and someone is liable to get angry or defensive. but why? nothing is fact and nothing is fiction. Everything we know, or think we know has no backing to it. Its all thoughts, opinions, and so called findings from someone else. so how are we to really know? Because some one is educated, they now have the say as to what is what and who is who? or maybe they themselves have no right because someone without education might know the real meanings, if there are "real" meanings. But who's to know? All the psychology that's out there, if you really look closely, you will see glitches. no one person agrees with another on it. there are too many different views, opinions, options. Freud fought himself on his own views as well as others. They say he was a sick man though. Why? because he knew so much? Or maybe his views weren't agreed upon nor accepted, so he got a label instead of an award. How do we know anything he says isn't true, whether or not he was mentally disabled. How are we to know if someone is mentally disturbed if no one really knows the true meaning but of what one says. But even than it's still fought upon till this day and more labels are coming out. Even labels have labels now. But why? because one is not smart enough to help one fit into society? or maybe they are too smart and take it too a level that doesn't exist. Because one has more energy than another, they are hyperactive? They are now labeled with ADD (attention deficit disorder). When one is smarter than another yet slower in "important" areas such as speech they are autistic. And because one appears different to one's eye and does not act the same as the other person, they now have down-syndrome. If someone isn't as tall as another, they are a midget. If One has a bad day and gets depressed and low, they are Bipolar. If one is nervous and acts nervous they have anxiety. Because one is paranoid and or thinks differently than another they are schizophrenic. one has Post Traumatic Stress Disorder because of trauma in their life and others don't find it "normal" how they live with it. One is wrong and banned because of beliefs because they believe something that another does not and now they too are labeled, terrorists. Some people are shy and don't agree with what some agree on and they are now Loners. Some express themselves through costume or dress but because not everyone does it or like it they are suicidal, Gothic or even a freak. Seeing a pattern yet? In today's society no matter what you are, who you are, what you do, how you act or what you achieve, there's something wrong with you. Why? because your not like the other. but nobody is like the other, so technically it should go like this... We all are nervous creatures who have bad days, even weeks who do get paranoid from time to time from events, and have intelligence on different levels as well and energy in different forms. We all look different and act different, dress different and expect different. we all have gone through or will go through traumatic experiences and deal with it differently than everyone else because were not someone else. We are born in ratios of pounds and inches and grow to be what we are whether its 4'2 or 7'0. We eat different foods and come from different backgrounds and believe different things. We all are lonely sometimes and don't agree with others on different things. We all will dress differently because we see things differently and like certain colors or styles while others don't and choose another. So basically what we have here.... The human Race. Or Maybe We Are All Crazy! but what is crazy, and what does it even mean? Like Normal, is there such a thing? who says what gets to be what, or who is what? are they right? If GOD wanted us to be all the same he wouldn't have punished Adam and Eve. He wouldn't have even made Eve. If He wanted us the same we would be the same and see the same. If He wanted labels he would've marked us himself. For once he was labeled and marked with a crown of thorns and thought of as "crazy." If we all thought the same, there would be nothing to talk about or learn let alone live for. But again, who am I to say anything? all I have is opinions just like everyone else. But maybe because I have opinions and what I feel is courage, that makes ME crazy. after all we all have to be labeled right?........ Next time you see someone, compliment them because their not you. Next time you label someone know what that label really means and make sure you've never felt that way, even once, or your labeling yourself... And next time you question something and wonder why, know there is no right or wrong answer and either way your going to find out your own answer. Or don't take anything I write into acknowledgment and don't do anything at all. But wont that make you lazy? or maybe just not intelligent and maybe even slow. so are you now "retarded?" If that word even exists. But again who am I to speak, but just another someone out there who thinks, talks, dresses, acts and believes different than others. Just another Human. and my words have no backing just like everyone else's. Expectations...what you think you might have, maybe its untrue, or maybe it is true. but who knows the levels of what's high or too low. What would make them right to say so? Is there even a such thing as expectation and how do you know? because someone said so...?

Reflections

Just Because you see an image, it doesn't mean what your seeing is what you're getting. It's just an image.. Isn't it true that a reflection is just that... a reflection? So what does reflection really mean?

"Reflection: The act of reflecting, turning, or sending back, or the state of being reflected. The return of rays, beams, sound, or the like, from a surface. The reverting of the mind to that which has already occupied it; meditation; contemplation; hence, also, that operation or power of the mind by which it is conscious of its own acts or states; the capacity for judging rationally, especially in view of a moral rule or standard."

"Never judge a book by it's cover" It's amazing how the mind works... But one of our biggest weaknesses is how it tricks us. you've heard that saying "the mind plays tricks on us." It's a lot truer than I believe YOU think it is... Just remember that next time you open your eyes... Decide what Reflection you want, because in the end.. that's all that counts.

Have Faith and Believe...

When you think enough is enough, and your ready to give up, take my advice...Take a step back, think, pray and than Push harder than you ever thought you could. In the end, you will not only get the result(s) you want, but you will get rewarded with more than you thought you could have.

Make Giving up an option that is not available to you. Make your back a support for those to lean on, and have another back for you to lean on when needed. Give back to those who have ever helped, and help them even when not asked. Remember who you are, and never let anyone make you doubt it or the strength you possess. Know your weaknesses and remember we all have them, its to know how to get around them and get through them that make the difference.

Love all without hate, because to hate is to care, and why waste a feeling that could be put to better use. Always remember that no matter how hard you think life can be, you have the strength needed to proceed. God would never throw something your way if he didn't think you can handle it. I now know that He does what He does to test your belief and to give you strength. it back to him. A test of Faith. And when you think of it, how many have failed. I know I can count more people than on both hands and that saddens me. But it also makes me realize on how miserable their life will be in the end because who else is there that possess the most strength and all the answers/keys to our challenges. God. so without belief, without faith you won't get to far in your journey. I know from everything I have gone through in my life, and I can say with certainty that I have been through the worst, I have never given up or lost my faith in God. I won't lie and say I never thought of giving up, or just quitting. I've been to that point. Just today I felt at that point, but whenever I do feel like that I step back. literally. I close my eyes and bow my head and I say a prayer. I ask for help and I put my pride aside. and than I make the sign of the cross for confirmation to myself that it goes through (like mail). My outcome with that has always been positive. When asked, God has always sent me what I need, want, or even just a sign to let me know that not only could I do it, get through it, or beat it, but that he is near and will guide me where I need to go. I've never once had him not be there for me because I Believe.

You have to have Faith. God gave us life and he can take it away just as easily. Jesus died on the cross for us and he never even knew us, just those who hated him, Mary was punished to lose her husband through disbelief and her son through hatred of who he was and who he said he was from. With all that, we honestly face nothing compared to what could be. We have to remember that , and face the fact that we have it better than we give credit for. I believe today was for me to speak of this and to share with you how important it is to Believe. We all have an angel, a guardian angel, an arc-angel, a spiritual guide, an animal guide, 4 sacred eyes, and So much more I could name. The point though is why do we have all these if God didn't care Why would he make sure that each one of us would be cared for, loved, watched over, and guided. Put it all together and look at your life. Look at the times you wonder how you made it through. Look at the times you know you shouldn't be alive for. Look at the times you think you never would've had.... When you think enough is enough, think this... Enough of that situation, let me change gears and go with my faith and Believe that I can get through this.

True Pain..

I should think that pain, like anything else that can affect the mind and heart, can be a permanent mark. I compare it to a scar. Scar's fade, but they never go away permanently. They are a reminder of what was and what is. and shouldn't it be that way? Because sometimes don't we need that reminder? that kick in the butt, if you will, to remember what got us to where we are today? and what will bring us to our tomorrow. I suppose it also depends on the pain spoken of. But in general isn't it all the same. whether it's a small thing, or a large matter, whether it was physical, or mental, whether it was meant or accidental, It still comes down to the same.

Pain hurts. and it hurts mostly in our hearts. I've endured my fair share. And in every department I can say. Since the day I was born I feel as though I have endured something at every age, and keep on enduring more and more as time goes on.

How much can one take until breaking point? How much is too much and when is enough, enough! I have come so far in my life. done so much and lived hard and to the fullest of my ability. not many can say they have experienced, let alone done half of what I have in their lifetime. I pride myself in that. I pride myself in never falling, never giving up, never backing down, never giving in, and never losing sight. I've never taken

advantage of situations. I've never blinded myself to truths. even with my ex I never told myself I was stupid for staying. I stayed for me, I don't quit and run. I did what I did to get through what I had to and I believe in my heart God was testing me if I was strong enough and willing enough to have my son, and I passed that test. I passed it and now I have my baby boy and the trials he goes through, we do together.

I will never let my son suffer. What parent would willingly? I will push on because that's just who I am, but I won't lie and say I'm perfect. I won't say I'm not tired because I'm very tired. I won't say I'm not frustrated because you wouldn't understand the frustration I deal with. I won't even say I'm not happy. I'm happy with who I am and where I have come from. But I will say that I too feel I need a break.

know what you have. forget what you don't have. appreciate, care, and walk away from what doesn't matter. Life is not a never ending story. it does have an ending, we just fill in the story. Enjoy what you can and make what you can't. If you can walk, walk. if you can live, live to your fullest and remember that to "the" fullest is not yours. make your own. Never take advantage, believe in karma when one does wrong, never let anyone bring you down, or not care for you the way you should and need to be cared for. nothing is enough. no such thing. it should be More than enough, always. You should always be more than enough, because each one of us is more than just individuals. were special and unique. Make yourself that much more and go the extra mile. And never feel ashamed to feel emotions. "There is no comfort if there is no pain."

Believe.

Believe, not only in yourself, but in your guide, your spirit, and your angel. Believe that when you need a shoulder, one is there for you, you need only to lean. And believe that what you want and need to accomplish, will be. Have faith, have patience and be yourself. It will all come together. I believe that we all have a path that we take in life and here's how I see it and how I believe it to be....

God gives us two options, or paths. One path leads us down a journey to where we are supposed to be at that given time. No obstacles just a free ride. the other path has the same destination... BUT here's where it gets rocky. The second path is the one we take when we are not ready mentally or physically to get to the destination that is next for us. It takes us through obstacles and the "that rocky road" to prepare and guide us for the next step. Think about this.. you ever feel like it took forever for you to get what you wanted in certain areas or certain things.. or what about with jobs, love, or even just the healing process. Seems like we take this long journey to finally get through what we need to get through in order to endure our next step.

Now think about this... what if we always got what we wanted at the time we wanted it. It would never last would it. we would never be fully prepared to take it on, nor would we be able to hold on to it, it would slip through our fingers and we would be left with nothing. So when you feel as though nothing is going right, nothing is as it should be, or that you feel alone and lost..., know this... your never wrong, your never where you shouldn't be, and your never alone (we all have our angels and guardians) At some point you will reach your destination. The whole idea is to BELIEVE.

Its those who give up, those who do not believe any longer, and take the easy way that fail the fastest and are the most miserable. They are not patient nor do they want or plan to be. It's those who think they will make it to the top but eventually fall straight toward the bottom and blame everyone else for their down fall. Do you want this to be you? or do you want to believe and go through and endure what you need to in order to succeed and get the most out of life.

What we also forget is that through our trials and stipulations, we still have moments. Moments that we never forget, moments we hold on too, and moments that mean so much to us. And most of all we have the moments that build and mold us into who and what we are today.

Strength is not given, it is earned. You cannot walk out your house one day with the strength to endure something you have never endured before, nor will you walk out as a success. Ironically it will turn into a disaster. You earn strength from building yourself from your falls. From picking yourself up when you think you can't go anymore. You receive and feel it when you have gotten through the things we always think we can't get through, and walk out with another notch under our belt. When things get tough I see people go two different ways. I see runners. now when I say runner I don't mean they ran from just one thing, I mean the ones who run from the whole situation and never look back; thinking it would not follow them. They learn the hard way that whatever you leave behind, always catches up, but builds its own strength while catching up to you. Then there are those who face things head on. we all have a different way of doing it, but that's not really the point. The point would be to face the situation, problem or question and tackle it head on with everything you've got. Make yourself that much stronger, that much wiser so that the next time your put on the line for a life test, you will be able to do it without much thought.

Jealousy, Hatred and Starting Over..

I know of all of the above and have felt them at one time or another. We all have. But when is it time to move on and just be?,... because your now stepping into the territory of "Enough is Enough." Jealousy is one of the most heard of besides hatred. But how often do you see people affected by hate.. And how many do you see affected by jealousy. To hate is to feel, to have emotion(s) towards someone enough to show that even if you hate someone, you care enough to feel that away. Most people bypass this with jealousy.

Being jealous of someone(s) doesn't involve emotions although people may differ their opinion of this, but than I will put it this way.. if you have emotions towards someone it is not jealousy, it runs a lot deeper.. Jealousy is simple. It's a feeling. Not an emotion. It's a feeling of basic failure within yourself on or in whatever it may be your being jealous towards. For example: Simple. A girl in school got new shoes, you can't afford to. your jealous because they got to have something you wanted and can't get yourself. intermediate: A girl got the guy you have wanted to date. Your jealous because you didn't have the balls yourself to get him for yourself and now you lost your chance. Heavy: This is where "enough is enough" comes in: someone has been able to do something that you couldn't and you resent them for it. so you make it a project to make them feel miserable when in truth the real miserable person is yourself. I can't tell you how often I have seen this. I've had it happen to me more than once. It's almost ridiculous but its so severe to the point of one person can drive another to suicide. I've seen it done and I resent that in its own.

What people don't understand is that the people who try to make other's miserable are trying to make themselves feel better about themselves.

Be Careful What you Wish for...

Nothing is as what is seems. We live in illusions. What people don't understand and will never grasp is that Control is a word that is non-existent. Look over every situation and think of when you ever had control over something or someone. You never did nor will you ever. Control is an illusion we give ourselves to feel more powerful but in reality everything we have can slip away just as easy as a snap of the fingers. so when you wish, make sure you know what and why you are wishing and hold on to it knowing you can never control it.

I remember that and I've applied it to everything in my life. Its not only true but its scary because obtaining something can be so hard, but keeping it.. its even harder sometimes. We wish everyday for something in our lives. Its a simple fact. But do we realize half the time what were wishing for? are we ready for it? and if we obtain that wish.. are we willing to fight to keep it: because controlling it isn't an option.

When I was little I wished for so many things. and as time went by it always changed. the simple growing up I guess you would say. When you lose someone you love, it is so powerful, you never come to accept that they are gone. you think you do, but you really don't. you always have the why? the what? and the what if's, But what if we look at it a bit differently?

we all are selfish creatures. when we don't get what we want we never take it lightly. when we do we don't appreciate and really know what we have. "You don't know what you have until it is gone. "But even than I really don't think we knew what we had, just the illusion that we could've had something if we realized what it really was. but in actuality now you will never know, and we don't take that to acceptance.

So now what if you finally get what you wished for, what you've always wanted and never thought you would get.. and you have no idea what to do because you feel like with just a snap of the fingers... it could be gone.

Now imagine this: What you say is always wrong or ridiculous. What you do is always unacceptable. how you are is never enough and how you look is never good enough. And everything you are or ever were is now gone because you lost it, trying so hard to be what that person wanted. to please them, you have finally now lost everything you ever were and now start from scratch. what would you find? how would you do it? and what would it be like?

Imagine looking in the mirror and thinking I don't know you. the reflection is someone so far gone and lost you have no idea who you are staring at. But knowing you have to do something about it. Knowing you have to build someone from that. Now I see: A strong person who can weather a storm if needed and comfort when asked. I can get through tough and stick to sweet. I can fight when needed but walk away when it's not worth my time. I am me, a person I built from nothing and now have everything.

When I wish I wish big. meaning I hardly wish but if I do or when I do its for a great reason. I don't wish for the next hot car, or a great shopping spree, I wish for true love. I wish for health. I wish for tranquility for my family and resolution none of us have been able to find within each other. I wish with all my heart that the people I have lost rest comfortably and are in the hands of GOD and enjoying there latte's up there in heaven. I wish for peace between people because of the drama that's created on a daily basis is breaking everyone apart.

"To love is not to conquer; but in fact to face your biggest fear; Losing"

Is Seeing Really Believing

When was the last time you took a good look at yourself and your surroundings and really realized all that you have? Why does it always seem like its not enough or never enough, until you have nothing left at all, but a realization that you did, at one point, have everything you ever needed.

We Knit pick. we criticize. We judge. We name/label. We even put down. But when was the last time you said something nice to a person that needed to hear it? When was the last time you helped out when you weren't even asked but knew you should? And when was the last time you looked at yourself and realized that all the criticizing and judging was always about yourself and never really about anyone else.

We can have perfect eye sight and yet never see a damn thing. why is that? why do we walk around with our "eyes wide shut." Those of you know the saying understand. for those who don't let me explain. I'll start with, the way I learned the saying "eyes wide shut" was from my father. he told me on many occasions, "Alicia you can see everything and anything you want to see, but you can't have your eyes closed. you have to be able to look at it all and see the big picture to understand the little ones and make sense of their surroundings; Otherwise you are walking around with your eyes wide shut." When I said... "WHAT?" (I was only 9) he laughed and said "you will understand one day when you have to see something you never wanted to see before." I'll never forget my first time of experiencing that, and because of that I will never forget or live any other way but with the ability to see everything as a whole and not just the small pictures that surround it.

Without Love; We are without Light

~Remember that without love there is no light, and without light there is no meaning to life.~

For the past 3 years and 9 months I have put all my time and energy on 2 things. My son being number one,(priority, responsibility and love), and advancing in my career/work. In between those two things I left no time for much else besides the occasional friends getting together, or the "dating" scene which, to my liking, never worked out. After my ex husband and I broke apart, and this was years before the divorce, I always went with the belief that I will never love again, I will never be with a man that way again. That I could never "feel again." I believed strongly , and maybe it was just convincing myself, but I believed that he was my soul mate, and that was it for me. there would never be any body else. Through out the years, it never bothered me because being a single mom, the last worry on your mind is when your next date is, or who your next lover will be. Not to mention I worked so hard with my career, education, my home and my son, that it just never was a thought I questioned.

I'm not saying I didn't go on the occasional dates here and there, but they never went anywhere after that. I always enjoy being taking to dinner, I'm an old school romantic so I can never turn that down, but other than that, nothing else appealed. I would and could find any or every flaw on the guy I was with and that was excuse enough for me not to do it again.

When I enter anything... a job, a position, a relationship, whatever it may be, I give 110%. I always believed and know that it takes 55% on both parts to make anything work. You must be able to have your heart open to possibilities, which includes vulnerability.

Do I believe in love? Yes of course. I never said I didn't love my ex-husband.

I always will in a crazy way. We said vows once upon a time and he gave me a precious gift, my son. Everything else is his to deal with because I did all I could do. I was able to walk away knowing I did everything I could to make us work. But sometimes we have to part with that knowledge alone and heal. People don't change but they do have choices.

One day I will have what I need and want, but for now I'm content with what I have. Just remember that everyone asks and thinks the same things when leaving a relationship. "Will I ever love again, will I ever find anyone, am I good enough, who will date me now, will the sex be as good, and what if I never find someone…" Its all normal. Its vulnerability and fear. It just makes you human.

Mirror Image..

Have you yet to take a step back to look at yourself in a way others perceive you? Have you ever wondered what it would be like to see yourself from another persons eyes? And if you had the ability, what would You want to see?

I have imagined many times what people see when they look at me. I know they see a woman but at the same time they see a girl. some people would tell you they see strength where others would tell you they see fear. I know for sure people would tell you that their initial feeling after seeing and/or meeting me is intimidation.

When you have confidence and you walk with your head up high, people seem to find themselves in a dilemma of trust. They usually will tell you they find two thoughts pop into their heads; one saying this person is strong and powerful, or two, a feeling of intimidation and no ability to see through that. When someone is able to look into another's eyes, they usually can see everything they need to know about that person. We believe ourselves to be armored and closed up tight. Its an amazing thing to be able to read a persons eyes, body language and the signals they put out if you are trained to. But if you are not, your just judging without the right to do so. That's where we go wrong most of the time and people jump to conclusions. It's easier to give a person a name or label than to get to know who they really are.

No one should feel anything less than a positive feeling toward them, unless they earned a negative reaction. Even so, nobody has the right for that either in my opinion. Sometimes I feel as though when people look at me they see two options clearly. To be my friend, or to be my enemy. Why? Well its elemental. My professor once told me its a primal instinct that I give out to make such an intimidating presence. for example: I am like a wolf and everything that sees me is like that of another breed, some more powerful and some less. The wolf is a powerful creature than has no fears and always looks straight ahead even when they hear a noise in the brush. I work the same way. Its not just me, its all of us and the way we tend to perceive and move too fast.

I hear the talk, the criticizing, I even hear the drama. But I still walk with my eyes straight ahead and my head held up high; and I never look back or around to see who's lurking there. It's not worth my time and never will be. We should only worry about the things that will benefit us, not the petty feelings or assumptions people make on you. I just feel that if we as humans are given one life, than we have one chance, one opportunity to live out that life. To me, if you look back, that is time in your life that was wasted.

No matter who and/or what you are, you have no reason to look back. you have no reason to listen and you have no reason to let elements affect you. the only person that can do that is yourself. Your worst enemy and worst critic is you. If you know and feel your good enough and have confidence, the rest just flows. And isn't that how we all want to live? I ask you to try this the next time you think you have something to look back at... Don't. Keep on going. Don't let whatever it may be affect you in any way. Know what the feeling is to be able to keep going and not care, and I guarantee the next time, you will not only do it automatically, but you skip a moment lost of your life being brought down with a negative. We all deserve the best, so why not give each other just that?

Quantity or Quality...

What I never understood, and probably never will, is why people pretend to be someone or something they are not. Also known as "fake" people. The thing is, after a certain period of time doing this, you really do lose your identity as to who you were to begin with.

The major problem that I've seen and heard is that people never feel good enough or important enough. But who really knows what is good enough? Do you know how transparent you are? Ask yourself how many times you've called a person fake. Now what makes you think they can't see that your fake (if you are acting fake)? So really, your just a walking label and a hypocrite.

Society, as we know, has all of us believe that if your not a certain way, your unacceptable. Also when one is labeled, everyone will use that label against you as well. And its not only fake. There's now "emo" which was when I went to high school was also know as gothic. And so on. Point being these people are carrying a name because of how they act and dress. But what about what they think?

How far will you go to fit in. How much will you listen to join a crowd. and how many will you hurt to find a spot. Do you understand that in the long run, you will be left with no one and nothing. We always go to another crowd or another way but not always will you be accepted.

"Its Quality over Quantity," this is what I grew up on and will always believe. That's how I choose to live. Wouldn't you want to know who is your best friend? Who will be there for you through the worst and get you through it, and who will be there through the best when you need to share. Who will never label you, because to them your you and nothing else. And to know that no matter what the next day brings, their still your friend till the end. That's what I call being true. What true is and should be is what matters most. So ask yourself a few questions and see what you are.. I bet what you thought you were, is not who you really are deep inside or who you want to be.

Remember this, if you are called a name, labeled or deemed as not good enough, the person or persons saying these things are really talking about themselves in who they really are . Nobody knows the "true" you except for yourself. Sometimes we forget that, but know it's what impact we make with it that counts, not what group we decided to join or follow.

Rhyme or Reason

Life. It can be either easy and worthless and hard and worth while. So just because someone picks one way doesn't make them wrong. They chose their own destination. We all have reasons. They should be our own and no one else's, but unfortunately it doesn't
always go that way.

Most of our actions come from sources. When was the last time you got angry and freaked out because you were sitting alone relaxing? It doesn't happen. If you'd like to get technical it can happen yes, but what were you thinking about while you were "relaxing." Getting mad has to come from an outside source. Anger is an emotion just like sadness or happiness. Emotions are our own but they are found from outside sources. An example: a friend comes over and gives you a hug. You find yourself feeling warm inside with happiness and content. The friend was the source; the content feeling was an emotion of happiness. The most common emotion misunderstood and disliked is fear. Fear is actually not an emotion, but it stems from an emotion. We are born with no fear. We take on the world with eyes open and heads up. As we grow, we start to gain fears from things, people, movies, songs, environment and so on. There's no rhyme or reason to it, its how our genetic makeup is composed. If we were perfect, we would be emotionless, which can be a nice thought sometimes but we also would know no boundaries.

Emotions lead us to a safe place whether you know it or not. If you fear heights, its for a reason. Someone does not walk off a 20 story building for no reason. There was boundaries that were crossed. What about drowning, or even something as simple as sadness or anger. We repress our anger most of the time because its not good in our society to walk around with it. How many people, that you know, have either broken down, or freaked out completely due to keeping or holding their anger in? And where do you think anxiety stems from?

We always cross boundaries; sometimes we never cross them, but there is no stepping in the middle of one. Its one or the other. Its amazing how every single one of us is so different. We each posses qualities that are uniquely our own and will always be our own. Don't let anyone take that from you. You are who you are and that will never change. The only thing to change is how you think, or how you feel about "who you are." It's than that you will find your right "emotion", or your "rhyme and reason."

Anxiety.

<hr />

The pain and fear that come along with anxiety are not something to consider lightly. Anxiety is a feeling of nervousness, but leads into anxiety attacks, commonly known as panic attacks. They hit hard and they hit fast without warning. No one has really discovered the perfect cure for anxiety but it stems from something else. Such as depression, fears, post traumatic stress disorder, manic depression, and so on. It could be as simple as having a trauma happen and leaving you with having panic attacks as the result of it.

Its hard, not only to understand but to explain it and when you do people never look at you right. Not that you sound crazy but that you are making it up, or making it worse than it is.

The usual panic attack consists of difficulty in breathing, rapid heart beat, a feeling of fear or uneasiness, sometimes fainting or blacking out. They compare the feeling closely to having a heart attack. The reality of it is that its your mind taking over and you letting it. It is you being overwhelmed or letting a fear getting to you to the point of not having "control" anymore.

When having an attack the best thing to do is keep talking to yourself. Talk yourself through it and out of it. I thought it was nuts when I was told that but I have used that technique along with anger and it has never failed me. What you need to do is make yourself understand when the attack first comes on that you have control. Tell yourself that. Tell yourself to slow your breathing and calm your heartbeat. Remind yourself over and over, until you believe, that it is in fact all in your head and its is NOT real. Because it isn't real. And that's where I am at. When I feel one coming on, I remind myself it is not real, and that I do have the ability to make it end. Than I go back and try to figure out why it was ready to come on the way it did. Something always triggers an attack. that's another thing to realize. Seeing something, hearing, feeling, its always part of your five senses.

There is nothing wrong with you. Its just a way for your mind to react in fear instead of your body reacting. It will get better. That is a promise I can make to you if your willing to work through it. But remember nothing is instant. Time heals all.

If I can say one thing that has helped me the most, its when I feel one come on, I get angry. By bringing in another emotion it confuses the mind which voids the attack but while I get angry I justify it by saying "No, I'm not having an attack because it is NOT REAL and I won't allow it anymore." and if I have to keep saying it I will. If I have to say it aloud I will. There is always tricks to it, you will find yours.

A few thoughts of Belief

~A Birth Certificate shows that we were born.
~A Death Certificate shows that we died .
~Pictures show that we lived!
~We dictate what we believe; Life only shows us examples.

I Believe...
That just because two people argue,
It doesn't mean they don't love each other.
And just because they don't argue,
It doesn't mean they do love each other.

I Believe...
That we don't have to change friends if
We understand that friends change.

I Believe....
That no matter how good a friend is,
they're going to hurt you every once in a while
and you must forgive them for that.

I Believe...
That true friendship continues to grow,
even over the longest distance.
Same goes for true love.

I Believe...
That you can do something in an instant
That will give you heartache for life.

I Believe....
That it's taking me a long time
To become the person I want to be
But worth every moment.

I Believe...
That you should always leave loved ones with
Loving words. It may be the last time you see them.

I Believe....
That you can keep going long after you think you can't.

I Believe....
That we are responsible for what
We do, no matter how we feel.

I Believe...
That either you control your attitude or it controls you.

I Believe...
That heroes are the people who do what has to be done when it needs
to be done, regardless of the consequences.

I Believe....
That my best friend and I can do anything or nothing and have the best time.

I Believe....
That sometimes the people you expect to kick you when you're down
will be the ones to help you get back up.

I Believe...
That sometimes when I'm angry
I have the right to be angry,
But that doesn't give me the right to be cruel.

I Believe....
That maturity has more to do with what types of experiences you've had
And what you've learned from them and less to do with how many
birthdays you've celebrated.

I Believe....
That it isn't always enough,
to be forgiven by others.
Sometimes, you have to learn to forgive yourself.

I Believe...
That no matter how bad your heart is broken
the world doesn't stop for your grief.

I Believe....
That our background and circumstances
may have influenced who we are,
But, we are responsible for who we become.

I Believe...
That you shouldn't be so eager to find
Out a secret. It could change your life Forever.

I Believe....
Two people can look at the exact same
Thing and see something totally different.

I Believe...
That your life can be changed in a matter of minutes or
Hours by people who don't even know you.

I Believe...
That even when you think you have no more to give,
When a friend cries out to you -
you will find the strength to help.

I Believe...
That credentials on the wall
do not make you a decent human being.

I Believe...
That the people you care about most in life
are taken from you too soon.

Make the most of all that life gives you.